Spurgeon's Sermons
on
Soulwinning

C. H. Spurgeon Sermon Series

Spurgeon's Sermons on Soulwinning

CHARLES HADDON SPURGEON

kregel
PUBLICATIONS

Grand Rapids, MI 49501

Spurgeon's Sermons on Soulwinning
by Charles H. Spurgeon.

Copyright © 1995 by Kregel Publications.

Published by Kregel Publications, a division of Kregel, Inc.,
P.O. Box 2607, Grand Rapids, MI 49501. Kregel
Publications provides trusted, biblical publications for
Christian growth and service. Your comments and sug-
gestions are valued.

Cover artwork: Don Ellens
Cover and book design: Alan G. Hartman

Library of Congress Cataloging-in-Publication Data

Spurgeon, C. H. (Charles Haddon), 1834–1892.
   [Sermons on soulwinning]
   Spurgeon's Sermons on Soulwinning / by Charles H.
Spurgeon.
      p.   cm.
    1. Evangelistic work—Sermons. 2. Sermons, English.
3. Baptists—Sermons. I. Title. II. Series: Spurgeon,
C. H. (Charles Haddon), 1834–1892. C. H. Spurgeon
sermon series.
BV3797.S648   1994   252'.3—dc20   94-40572
                                           CIP

ISBN 0-8254-3787-3 (pbk.)

2 3 4 5 printing / year 99 98

Printed in the United States of America

Contents

"Analyze the gifts of that powerful evangelist as accurately as you can; measure, as closely as may be possible, the secret of his influence; but I do not believe that you will find any other teacher whose printed sermons would be read week after week, year after year, by tens and hundreds of thousands, not only all over England, Scotland, and Wales, but in the backwoods of Canada, on the prairies of America, in the remotest settlements of Australia and New Zealand, wherever an English newspaper can reach, or the English tongue is spoken. The thing is absolutely unique. It has no parallel. . . . What was it that gave [Spurgeon] a religious influence so unparalleled in our day, and made his name a household word all over the wide world? No doubt he had rare gifts. He was courageous, resolute, and lively in these times of the faint heart, irresolution and dullness. He had that genuine eloquence which is all the more effective because of its directness and simplicity. He had a matchless voice, powerful and vibrating with every quality of earnestness and variety. He had humor, tender pathos, and never failed to be interesting. He was utterly untrammelled by the questionings of criticism. But it was, above all, the splendid completeness, the unswerving strength, the exuberant vitality of his faith in God's revelation to man through His Son Jesus Christ, combined with the width and warmth of his zealous love for souls, that gave him that unbounded power which he exercised so loyally for Christian belief. . . ."

Archdeacon Sinclair of St. Paul's Cathedral
on the impact of Spurgeon's ministry

1
Soulwinning

He that winneth souls is wise (Proverbs 11:30).

The text does not say, "He that winneth sovereigns is wise," though no doubt *he* thinks himself wise, and perhaps, in a certain groveling sense in these days of competition, he must be so; but such wisdom is of the earth, and ends with the earth; and there is another world where the currencies of Europe will not be accepted, nor their past possession be any sign of wealth or wisdom. Solomon, in the text before us, awards no crown for wisdom to crafty statesmen, or even to the ablest of rulers; he issues no diplomas even to philosophers, poets, or men of wit; he crowns with laurel only those who win souls. He does not declare that he who preaches is necessarily wise—and alas! there are multitudes who preach, and gain much applause and eminence, who win no souls, and who shall find it goes hard with them at the last, because in all probability they have run and the Master has never sent them. He does not say that he who talks about winning souls is wise, since to lay down rules for others is a very simple thing, but to carry them out oneself is far more difficult. He who actually, really, and truly turns men from the error of their ways to God, and so is made the means of saving them from going down to hell, is a wise man; and that is true of him whatever his style of soulwinning may be. He may be a Paul, deeply logical, profound in doctrine, able to command all candid judgments; and if he thus wins souls he is wise. He may be all Apollos, grandly rhetorical, whose lofty genius soars into the very heaven of eloquence; and if he wins souls in that way he is wise, but not otherwise. Or he may be a Cephas, rough and rugged, using uncouth metaphor and stern declamation, but if he win souls he is no less wise than his polished brother or his argumentative friend, but not else. The great wisdom of soulwinners, according to the text, is proven only by their

This sermon was taken from *The Metropolitan Tabernacle Pulpit* and was preached in January of 1869.

actual success in really winning souls. To their own Master they are accountable for the ways in which they work, not to us. Do not let us be comparing and contrasting this minister and that. Who are you that judge another man's servants? Wisdom is justified in all her children. Only children wrangle about incidental methods; men look at sublime results. Do these workers of many sorts and divers manners win souls? Then they are wise, and you who criticize them, being yourselves unfruitful, cannot be wise, even though you affect to be their judges. God proclaims soul-winners to be wise, dispute it who dare. This degree from the College of Heaven may surely stand them in good stead, let their fellow mortals say what they will of them.

"He that winneth souls is wise," and this can be seen very clearly. He must be a wise man in even ordinary respects who can by grace achieve so divine a marvel. Great soulwinners never have been fools. A man whom God qualifies to win souls could probably do anything else which Providence might allot him. Take Martin Luther! Why, sirs, the man was not only fit to work a Reformation, but he could have ruled a nation or have commanded an army. Think of Whitfield, and remember that the thundering eloquence which stirred all England was not associated with a weak judgment, or an absence of brainpower; the man was a master orator, and if he had addicted himself to commerce would have taken a chief place among the merchants, or had he been a politician, amid admiring senates would have commanded the listening ear. He that wins souls is usually a man who could have done anything else if God had called him to it. I know the Lord uses what means He wills, but He always uses means suitable to the end; if you tell me that David slew Goliath with a sling, I answer—it was the best weapon in the world to reach so tall a giant, and the very fittest weapon that David could have used, for he had been skilled in it from his youth up. There is always an adaptation in the instruments which God uses to procure the ordained result, and though the glory is not to them, nor the excellence in them, but all is to be ascribed to God, yet is there a fitness and preparedness which God sees, even if we do not. It is assuredly true that soulwinners are by no means idiots or simpletons, but such as God makes wise for Himself, though vainglorious wiseacres may dub them fools.

"He that winneth souls is wise," because he has selected a wise object. I think it was Michelangelo who once carved certain magnificent statues in snow. They are gone; the material readily compacted by the frost as readily melted in the heat. Far wiser was he when he fashioned the enduring marble, and produced works which will last all down the ages. But even marble itself is consumed and fretted by the tooth of time; and he is wise who selects for his raw material immortal souls, whose existence shall outlast the stars. If God shall bless us to the winning of souls, our work shall remain when the wood, and hay, and stubble of earth's art and science shall have gone to the dust from which they sprang. In heaven itself, the soulwinner, blessed of God, shall have memorials of his work preserved forever in the galleries of the skies. He has selected a wise object, for what can be wiser than to glorify God, and what, next to that, can be wiser than in the highest sense to bless our fellow men: to snatch a soul from the gulf that yawns, to lift it up to the heaven that glorifies; to deliver an immortal from the thralldom of Satan, and to bring him into the liberty of Christ? What more excellent than this? I say, that such an aim would commend itself to all right minds, and that angels themselves may envy us poor sons of men that we are permitted to make this our life object, to win souls for Jesus Christ. Wisdom herself assents to the excellence of the design.

To accomplish such a work, a man must be wise, for to win a soul requires infinite wisdom. God Himself wins not souls without wisdom, for the eternal plan of salvation was dictated by an infallible judgment, and in every line of it infinite skill is apparent. Christ, God's great soulwinner, is "the wisdom of God," as well as "the power of God." There is as much wisdom to be seen in the new creation as in the old. In a sinner saved, there is as much of God to be beheld as in a universe rising out of nothing; and we, then, who are to be workers together with God, proceeding side by side with Him to the great work of soulwinning, must be wise too. It is a work which filled a Savior's heart—a work which moved the Eternal mind before ever the earth was. It is no child's play, nor a thing to be achieved while we are half asleep, nor to be attempted without deep consideration, nor to be carried on without gracious help from the only wise God, our Savior. The pursuit is wise.

Mark well, my brethren, that he who is successful in soulwinning, will prove to have been a wise man in the judgment of those who see the end as well as the beginning. Even if I were utterly selfish, and had no care for anything but my own happiness, I would choose, if I might, under God, to be a soulwinner, for never did I know perfect, overflowing, unutterable happiness of the purest and most ennobling order, until I first heard of one who had sought and found a Savior through my means. I recollect the thrill of joy which went through me! No young mother ever rejoiced so much over her firstborn child—no warrior was so exultant over a hard-won victory. Oh! the joy of knowing that a sinner once at enmity has been reconciled to God, by the Holy Spirit, through the words spoken by our feeble lips. Since then, by grace given to me, the thought of which prostrates me in self-abasement, I have seen and heard of, not hundreds only, but even thousands of sinners turned from the error of their ways by the testimony of God in me. Let afflictions come, let trials be multiplied as God wills, still this joy preponderates above all others, the joy that we are to God a sweet savor of Christ in every place, and that as often as we preach the Word, hearts are unlocked, bosoms heave with a new life, eyes weep for sin, and their tears are wiped away as they see the great Substitute for sin, and live. Beyond all controversy, it is a joy worth worlds to win souls, and, thank God, it is a joy that does not cease with this mortal life. It must be no small bliss to hear, as one wings his flight up to the eternal throne, the wings of others fluttering at one's side toward the same glory, and turning around and questioning them, to hear them say, "We are entering with you through the gates of pearl; you brought us to the Savior." To be welcomed to the skies by those who call us father in God—father in better bonds than those of earth, father through grace, and sire for immortality. It will be bliss beyond compare, to meet in yon eternal seats with those begotten of us in Christ Jesus, for whom we travailed in birth, until Christ was formed in them, the hope of glory. This is to have many heavens—a heaven in every one won for Christ; according to the Master's promise, they that turn many to righteousness, shall shine as the stars forever and ever.

I have said enough brethren, I trust, to make some of you desire to occupy the position of soulwinners, but before I further address myself to my text, I would like to remind you that the honor does not belong to ministers only; they may take their full share of it, but it belongs to everyone of you who have devoted yourselves to Christ: such honor have all the saints. Every man here, every woman here, every child here, whose heart is right with God, may be a soulwinner. There is no man placed by God's providence where he cannot do some good. There is not a glowworm under a hedge, but gives a needed light; there is not a laboring man, a suffering woman, a servant girl, a chimney sweeper, or a crossing sweeper, but what has opportunities for serving God, and what I have said of soulwinners belongs not to the learned doctor of divinity, or to the eloquent preacher alone, but to you all who are in Christ Jesus. You can each of you, if grace enable you, be thus wise, and win the happiness of turning souls to Christ through the Holy Spirit.

I am about to dwell upon my text in this way—"He that winneth souls is wise"; I shall, first, *make that fact stand out a little clearer by explaining the metaphor used in the text—winning souls*; then, secondly, *give you some lessons in the matter of soulwinning, through which I trust the conviction will be forced upon each believing mind that the work needs the highest wisdom.*

The Metaphor Used in the Text

First, let us consider the metaphor used in the text—"He that winneth souls is wise."

We use the word *win* in many ways. It is sometimes found in very bad company, in those games of chance, juggling tricks and sleight of hand, or thimblerigging (to use a plain word), which sharpers are so fond of winning by. I am sorry to say that much of legerdemain and trickery are to be met with in the religious world. Why, there are those who pretend to save souls by curious tricks, intricate maneuvers, and dexterous posture. A basin of water, a half dozen drops, certain syllables—heigh, presto!—the infant is a child of grace, and becomes a member of Christ and an inheritor of the kingdom of heaven. This aqueous regeneration surpasses my belief; it is a trick which I do not understand: the initiated only can perform the beautiful piece of magic, which excels anything ever attempted by the Wizard of the North. There is a way, too, of winning souls by laying hands upon heads, only the elbows of aforesaid hands must be encased in lawn, and then the machinery acts, and there is grace conferred by blessed fingers! I must confess I do not understand the occult science, but at this I need not wonder, for the profession of saving souls by such juggling can only be carried out by certain favored persons who have received apostolical succession direct from Judas Iscariot. This episcopal confirmation, when men pretend that it confers grace, is an infamous piece of juggling. The whole thing is an abomination. Only to think that in this nineteenth century there should be men who preach up salvation by sacraments, and salvation by themselves indeed! Why, sirs, it is surely too late in the day to come to us with this drivel! Priestcraft, let us hope, is an anachronism, and the sacramental theory out of date. These things might have done for those who could not read, and for the days when books were scarce, but ever since the day when the glorious Luther was helped by God to proclaim with thunderclaps the emancipating truth, "By grace are ye saved, through faith, and that not of yourselves, it is the gift of God," there has been too much light for these Popish owls. Let them go back to their ivy-mantled towers, and complain to the moon of those who spoiled of old their kingdom of darkness. Let shaven crowns go to Bedlam, and scarlet hats to the scarlet harlot, but let not Englishmen yield them respect. Modern Tractarianism is a bastard Popery, too mean, too shifty, too double-dealing to delude men of honest minds. If we win souls it shall be by other arts than Jesuits and shavelings can teach us. Trust not in any man who pretends to priesthood. Priests are liars by trade, and deceivers by profession. We cannot save souls in their theatrical way and do not want to do so, for we know that with such jugglery as that, Satan will hold the best hand, and laugh at priests as he turns the cards against them at the last.

How do we win souls, then? Why, the word *win* has a better meaning far. It is used *in warfare*. Warriors win cities and provinces. Now, to win a soul is a much more difficult thing than to win a city. Observe the earnest soulwinner at his work: how cautiously he seeks his great Captain's directions to know when to hang out the white flag to invite the heart to surrender to the sweet love of a dying Savior; when, at the proper time, to hang out the black flag of threatening, showing that if grace be not received, judgment will surely follow; and when to unfurl, with dread reluctance, the red flag of the terrors of God against stubborn, impenitent souls. The soulwinner has to sit down before a soul as a great captain before a walled town, to draw his lines of circumvallation, to cast up his entrenchments and fix his batteries. He must not advance too fast—he may overdo the fighting; he must not move too slowly, for he may seem not to be in earnest, and may do mischief. Then he must know which gate to attack—how to plant his guns at Ear-gate, and how to discharge them; how, sometimes, to keep the batteries going, day and night, with red-hot shot, if perhaps he may make a breach in the walls; at other times, to lay by and cease, and then, on a sudden, to open all the batteries with terrific violence, if peradventure he may take the soul by surprise or cast in a truth when it was not expected, to burst like a shell in the soul, and do damage to the dominions of sin. The Christian soldier must know how to advance by little and little—to sap that prejudice, to undermine that old enmity, to blow into the air that lust, and at the last, to storm the citadel. It is his to throw the scaling ladder up, and to have his ears gladdened as he hears a clicking on the wall of the heart, telling that the scaling ladder has grasped and has gained firm hold; and then, with his saber between his teeth, to climb up, and spring on the man, and slay his unbelief in the name if God, and capture the city, and run up the blood-red flag of the cross of Christ, and say, "The heart is won, won for Christ at last." This needs a warrior well trained—a master in his art. After many day's attack, many weeks of waiting, many an hour of storming by prayer and battering by entreaty, to carry the Malakoff of depravity, this is the work, this the difficulty. It takes no fool to do this. God's grace must make a man wise thus to capture Mansoul, to lead its captivity captive, and open wide the heart's gates that the Prince Immanuel may come in. This is winning a soul.

The word *win* was commonly used among the ancients, *to signify winning in the wrestling match.* When the Greek sought to win the laurel, or the ivy crown, he was compelled a long time before to put himself through a course of training, and when he came forth at last stripped for the encounter, he had no sooner exercised himself in the first few efforts than you saw how every muscle and every nerve had been developed in him. He had a stern opponent, and he knew it, and therefore left none of his energy unused. While the wrestling was going on you could see the man's eye, how he watched every motion, every feint of his antagonist, and how his hand, his foot, and his whole body were thrown into the encounter. He feared to meet with a fall; he hoped to give one to his foe. Now, a true soulwinner has often to come to close quarters with the devil within men. He has to struggle with their prejudice, with their love of sin, with their unbelief, with their pride, and then again, all of a sudden, to grapple with their despair; at one moment he strives with their self-righteousness, at the next moment with their unbelief in God. Ten thousand arts are used to prevent the soulwinner from being conqueror in the encounter, but if God has sent him he will never renounce his hold of the soul he seeks until he has a throw to the power of sin, and won another soul for Christ.

Besides that, there is another meaning to the word *win*, upon which I cannot expatiate here. We use the word, you know, in a softer sense than these which have been mentioned, *when we come to deal with hearts*. There are secret and mysterious ways by which those who love win the object of their affection, which are wise in their fitness to the purpose. I cannot tell you how the lover wins his fond one, but experience has probably taught you. The weapon of this warfare is not always the same, yet where that victory is won the wisdom of the means becomes clear to every eye. The weapon of love is sometimes a look, or a soft word whispered and eagerly listened to; sometimes it is a tear; but this I know, that we have, most of us in our turn, cast around another heart a chain which that other would not care to break, and which has linked us two in a blessed captivity which has cheered our lives. Yes, and that is very nearly the way in which we have to save souls. That illustration is nearer the mark than any of the others. Love is the true way of soulwinning, for when I spoke of storming the walls, and when I spoke of wrestling, those were but metaphors, but this is near the fact. We win by love. We win hearts for Jesus by love, by sympathy with their sorrow, by anxiety lest they should perish, by pleading with God for them with all our hearts that they should not be left to die unsaved, by pleading with them for God that, for their own sake, they would seek mercy and find grace. Yes, sirs, there is a spiritual wooing and winning of hearts for the Lord Jesus, and if you would learn the way, you must ask God to give you a tender heart and a sympathizing soul. I believe that much of the secret of soulwinning lies in having compassion, in having spirits that can be touched with the feeling of human infirmities. Carve a preacher out of granite, and even if you give him an angel's tongue, he will convert nobody. Put him into the most fashionable pulpit, make his elocution faultless, and his matter profoundly orthodox, but so long as he bears within his bosom a hard heart he can never win a soul. Soul-saving requires a heart that beats hard against the ribs. It requires a soul full of the milk of human kindness. this is the *sine qua non* of success. This is the chief natural qualification for a soulwinner, which, under God and blessed of Him, will accomplish wonders.

I have not looked at the Hebrew of the text, but I find—and you will find, who have margins to your Bibles—that it is, "He that *taketh* souls is wise," which word refers to fishing, or to bird-catching. Every Sunday when I leave my house, I cannot help seeing as I come along, men, with their little cages and their stuffed birds, trying all around the common, and in the fields, to catch poor little warblers. They understand the method of alluring and entrapping their little victims. soulwinners might learn much from them. We must have our lures for souls adapted to attract, to fascinate, to grasp.

We must go forth with our birdlime, our decoys, our nets, our baits, so that we may catch the souls of men. Their enemy is a fowler possessed of the basest and most astounding cunning; we must outwit him with the guile of honesty, the craft of grace. But the art is to be learned only by divine teaching, and herein we must be wise and willing to learn. Irving, I think it is, tells us of some three gentlemen who had read in Izaak Walton all about the delights of fishing. So they wanted to enter upon the same amusement, and accordingly they became disciples of the gentle art. They went into New York and bought the best rods and lines that could be purchased, and they found out the exact fly for the particular day or month, so that the fish might bite at once, and as it were fly into the basket with alacrity. They fished, and fished, and fished the livelong day, but the basket was empty. They were getting disgusted with a sport that had no sport in it, when a ragged boy came down from the hills, without shoes or stockings, and humiliated them to the last degree. He had a bit of a bough pulled from off a tree, and a piece of string, and a bent pin; he put a worm on it, threw it in, and out came a fish directly, as if it were a needle drawn to a magnet. In again went the line, and out came another fish, and so on, until his basket was quite full. They asked him how he did it. Ah! he said, he could not tell them that, but it was easy enough when you had the way of it. Much the same is it in fishing for men. Some preachers who have silk lines and fine rods preach very eloquently and exceedingly gracefully, but they never win souls. I know not how it is, but another man comes with very simple language, but with a warm heart, and, straightway, men are converted to God. Surely there must be a sympathy between the minister and the souls he would win. God gives to those whom He makes soulwinners a natural love to their work, and a spiritual fitness for it. There is a sympathy between those who are to be blessed and those who are to be the means of blessing, and very much by this sympathy, under God, souls are taken; but it is as clear as noonday, that to be a fisher of men a man must be wise. "He that winneth souls is wise."

Some Ways by Which Souls Are to Be Won

And now, brethren and sisters, you who are engaged in the Lord's work from week to week, and who seek to win men's souls to Christ, I am, in the second place, to illustrate this by telling you of some of the ways by which souls are to be won.

The preacher himself wins souls. I believe, best, when he believes in the reality of his work, *when he believes in instantaneous conversions*. How can he expect God to do what he does not believe God will do? He succeeds best who expects conversion every time he preaches. According to his faith so shall it be done to him. To be content without conversions is the surest way never to have them: to drive with a single aim entirely at the saving of souls is the surest method of usefulness. If we sigh and cry until men are saved, saved they will be.

He will succeed best, *who keeps closest to soul-saving truth.* Now, all truth is not soulsaving, though all truth may be edifying. He that keeps to the simple story of the cross tells men over and over again that whosoever believes in Christ is not condemned, that to be saved nothing is wanted but simple trust in the crucified Redeemer; he whose ministry is much made up of the glorious story of the cross, the sufferings of the dying Lamb, the mercy of God, the willingness of the great Father to receive returning prodigals; he who cries, in fact, from day to day, "Behold the Lamb of God, which taketh away the sin of the world," he is likely to be a soul-winner, especially if he adds to this much prayer for souls, much anxious desire that men may be brought to Jesus, and then in his private life seeks as much as in his public ministry to be telling out to others of the love of the dear Savior of men.

But I am not talking to ministers, but to you who sit in the pew, and there-fore to you let me turn myself more directly. Brothers and sisters, you have different gifts. I hope you use them all. Perhaps some of you, though mem-bers of the church, think you have none; but every believer has his gift, and his portion of work. What can you do to win souls? Let me recommend to those who think they can do nothing, *the bringing of others to hear the Word.* That is a duty much neglected. I can hardly ask you to bring anybody here, but many of you attend other places which are not perhaps half filled. Fill them. do not grumble at the small congregation, but make it larger. Take somebody with you to the very next sermon, and at once the congregation will be increased. Go up with the prayer that your minister's sermon may be blessed, and if you cannot preach yourselves, yet, by bringing others under the sound of the Word, you may be doing what is next best. This is a very commonplace and simple remark, but let me press it upon you, for it is of great practical value. Many churches and chapels which are almost empty might soon have large audiences if those who profit by the Word would tell others about the profit they have received, and induce them to attend the same ministry. Especially in this London of ours, where so many will not go up to the house of God—persuade your neighbors to come forth to the place of worship; look after them; make them feel that it is a wrong thing to stay at home on the Sunday from morning until night. I do not say upbraid them, that does little good; but I do say entice them, persuade them. Let them have your tickets for the Tabernacle, for instance, sometimes, or stand in the aisles yourself, and let them have your seats. Get them under the Word, and who knows what may be the result? Oh, what a blessing it would be to you if you heard that what you could not do, for you could scarcely speak for Christ, was done by your pastor, by the power of the Holy Spirit, through your inducing one to come within earshot of the Gospel!

Next to that, soulwinners, *try after the sermon to talk to strangers*. The preacher may have missed the mark—you need not miss it; or the preacher may have struck the mark, and you can help to make the impression deeper by a kind word. I recollect several persons joining the church who traced their conversion to the ministry in the Surrey Music Hall, but who said it was not that alone, but another agency cooperating therewith. They were fresh from the country, and some good man, I knew him well, I think he is in heaven now, met two of them at the gate, spoke to them, said he hoped they had enjoyed what they had heard; said he would be glad if they would drop into his house to tea; they did, and he had a word with them about the Master. The next Sunday it was the same, and at last, those whom the sermons had not much impressed, were brought to hear with other ears, until by and by, through the good old man's persuasive words, and the good Lord's gracious work, they were converted to God. There is a fine hunting ground here, and indeed in every large congregation for you who really want to do good. How many come into this house every morning and evening with no thought about receiving Christ. Oh! if you would all help me, you who love the Master, if you would all help me by speaking to your neighbors who sit near to you, how much might be accomplished! Never let anybody say, "I came to the Tabernacle three months, and nobody spoke to me," but do, by a sweet familiarity, which ought always to be allowable in the house of God, seek with your whole heart to impress upon your friends the truth which I can only put into the ear, but which God may help you to put into the heart.

Further, let me commend to you, dear friends, *the art of buttonholing acquaintances and relatives*. If you cannot preach to a hundred preach to one. Get a hold of the man alone, and in love, quietly and prayerfully, talk to him. "One!" say you. Well, is not one enough? I know your ambition, young man; you want to preach here, to these thousands; be content, and begin with the ones. Your Master was not ashamed to sit on the well and preach to one, and when He had finished His sermon He had done good to all the city of Samaria, for that one woman became a missionary to her friends. Timidity often prevents our being useful in this direction, but we must not give way to it; it must not be tolerated that Christ should be unknown through our silence, and sinners unwarned through our negligence. We must school and train ourselves, but force ourselves to the irksome task until it becomes easy. This is one of the most honorable modes of soulwinning, and if it requires more than ordinary zeal and courage, so much the more reason for our resolving to master it. Beloved, we must win souls, we cannot live and see men damned; we must have them brought to Jesus. Oh! then, be up and doing, and let none around you die unwarned, unwept, uncared for. A tract is a useful thing, but a living word is better. Your eye, and face, and voice will all help. Do not be so cowardly as to give a piece of paper where your own speech would be so much better. I charge you, attend to this, for Jesus' sake.

④ *Some of you could write letters for your Lord and Master.* To far-off friends a few loving lines may be most influential for good. Be like the men of Issachar, who handled the pen. Paper and ink are never better used than in soulwinning. Much has been done by this method. Could not you do it? Will you not try? Some of you, at any rate, if you could not speak or write much, ⑤ *could live much.* That is a fine way of preaching, that of preaching with your feet. I mean preaching by your life, and conduct, and conversation. That loving wife who weeps in secret over an infidel husband, but is always so kind to him; that dear child whose heart is broken with a father's blasphemy, but is so much more obedient than he used to be before conversion; that servant whom the master swears at, but whom he could trust with his purse, and the gold uncounted in it; that man in trade who is sneered at as a Presbyterian, but who, nevertheless, is straight as a line, and would not be compelled to do a dirty action, no, not for all the mint; these are the men and women who preach the best sermons; these are your practical preachers. Give us your holy living, and with your holy living as the leverage, we will move the world. Under God's blessing we will find tongues, if we can, but we need greatly the lives of our people to illustrate what our tongues have to say. The Gospel is something like an illustrated paper. The preacher's words are the text, but the pictures are the living men and women who form our churches; and as when people take up such a newspaper, they very often do not read the text, but they always look at the pictures—so in a church, outsiders may not come to hear the preacher, but they always consider, observe, and criticize the lives of the members. If you would be soulwinners, then, dear brethren and sisters, see that you live the Gospel. I have no greater joy than this, that my children walk in the truth.

One thing more, ⑥ *the soulwinner must be a master of the art of prayer.* You cannot bring souls to God if you go not to God yourself. You must get your battle-ax, and your weapons of war, from the armory of sacred communion with Christ. If you are much alone with Jesus, you will catch His Spirit; you will be fired with the flame that burned in His breast and consumed His life. You will weep with the tears that fell upon Jerusalem when He saw it perishing, and if you cannot speak so eloquently as He did, yet shall there be about what you say somewhat of the same power which in Him thrilled the hearts and awoke the consciences of men. My dear hearers, specially you members of the church, I am always so anxious lest any of you should begin to lie upon your oars, and take things easy in the matters of God's kingdom. There are some of you—I bless you, and I bless God at the remembrance of you—who are in season, and out of season, in earnest for winning souls, and you are the truly wise, but I fear there are others whose hands are slack, who are satisfied to let me preach, but do not preach themselves; who take these seats, and occupy these pews, and hope the cause goes well, but that is all they do. Oh, do let me see you all in earnest! A great host of four thousand members—what ought we not to do if we are all alive, and all in earnest! But such a host, without the spirit of enthusiasm, becomes a mere mob, an unwieldy mass, out of which mischief grows, and no good results arise. If you were all firebrands for Christ, you might set the nation on a blaze. If you were all wells of living water, how many thirsty souls might drink and be refreshed!

One thing more you can do. If some of you feel you cannot do much personally, *you can always help the College*, and there it is that we find tongues for the dumb. Our young men are called out by God to preach; we give them some little education and training, and then away they go to Australia, to Canada, to the islands of the sea, to Scotland, to Wales, and throughout England, preaching the Word; and it is often, it must be often, a consolation to some of you, to think that if you have not spoken with your own tongues as you desire, you have at least spoken by the tongues of others, so that through you the Word of God has been sounded abroad throughout all this region.

Beloved, there is one question I will ask, and I have done, and that is, *Are your own souls won?* You cannot win others else. Are you yourselves saved? My hearers, every one of you, under that gallery there, and you behind here, are you yourselves saved? What if this night you should have to answer that question to another and greater than I am? What if the bony finger of the last great orator should be uplifted instead of mine? What if his unconquerable eloquence should turn those bones to stone, and glaze those eyes, and make the blood chill in your veins? Could you hope, in your last extremity, that you were saved? If not saved, how will you ever be? When will you be saved if not now? Will any time be better than now? The way to be saved is simply to trust in what the Son of Man did when He became man, and suffered the punishment for all those who trust Him. For all His people, Christ was a substitute. His people are those who trust Him. If you trust Him, He was punished for your sins, and you cannot be punished for them, for God cannot punish sin twice, first in Christ, and then in you. If you trust Jesus, who now lives at the right hand of God, you are this moment pardoned, and you shall forever be saved. O that you would trust Him now! Perhaps it may be now or never with you. May it be now, even now, and then, trusting in Jesus, dear friends, you will have no need to hesitate when the question is asked, "Are you saved?" for you can answer, "Yes I am, for it is written, 'He that believeth in him is not condemned.'" Trust Him, trust Him now, and then God help you to be a soulwinner, and you shall be wise, and God shall be glorified.

2

The Model Soulwinner

There cometh a woman of Samaria to draw water: Jesus saith unto her, Give me to drink (John 4:7).

This was the beginning of that interesting conversation which not only blessed this woman, but has been a means of grace to many others ever since, for this chapter and the previous one must be looked upon as among the most soulwinning parts of God's Word. I suppose that every portion of Scripture has had its use in the experience of men and women, but these two chapters have very, very largely been blessed in the commencement of the divine life. Many have been led through the door of regeneration and the gateway of faith by the truth so plainly taught in them.

I shall not delay you with any preface, but shall take you at once to the subject mentioned in our text.

The Model Soulwinner

You have before you here, first, the model soulwinner. Jesus said to the woman of Samaria, "Give me to drink." I speak to many here who are wise to win souls. I hope that I also address many more who, although they have not yet learned this wisdom, are anxious, if possible, to be used of God to bless their fellow creatures. Here, then, is a perfect model for you; study it and copy it.

First, observe that our Savior, as the model soulwinner, was *not reserved and distant.* 'Jesus therefore, being wearied with his journey, sat thus on the well." If He had not been wonderfully anxious to win a soul, He would have kept Himself to Himself; and if this woman had spoken to Him, He would have answered her shortly, and have let her see that He did not desire any conversation with her. There is a way of being civil, but at

---

This sermon was taken from *The Metropolitan Tabernacle Pulpit* and was preach on Sunday evening, July 10, 1887.

the same time of repressing anything like familiar conversation. There are some persons who have great gifts of freezing; they can freeze you almost with a look. You never dare to speak to them again; in fact, you stand and wonder how you could ever have had the impertinence to address such exalted personages! They evidently live in a very distinct world from that in which your poor self resides; they could not sympathize with you, they are too good or too great, too clever or too capacious; and if you do not complain of their conduct, yet you give them a wide berth, and keep clear of them for the future, for they are not at all the sort of people that attract you. They repel you by their coldness, they are not magnets; or if so, they exercise the very opposite influence from that of attraction. Now, if any of you are in such a frame of mind as that, pray the Lord to bring you out of it; but do not attempt to do any good while you are in such a condition, for you might as well try to heat an oven with snowballs as to win souls for Christ with a distant, cold, dignified manner of speech. No, cast all that away; for nothing can render you so feeble, and so useless, as to cultivate anything like separateness from your fellows. Come close to the sinner, draw near to him or to her; show that you are not keeping yourself to yourself, but that you regard the person you are addressing as a brother, as one who will find in you a sympathizer, who is touched with the feeling of his infirmities, seeing that you have suffered in many points like as he has suffered, and are therefore on the same level, and desire to stand on the same platform with him, and to do him good. There was nothing stiff and starched about the Savior. He was the very reverse of that, and even children felt that they might go to Him freely. He was like a great harbor into which sailors run their ships in stress of weather; they feel as if it was made on purpose for them. The very look of Christ's face, the very glistening of His eyes, everything about Him made people feel that He did not live for Himself at all, but that He desired to bless others. There is the model soulwinner, therefore, for your imitation, in Jesus sitting on the well, and condescending even to speak to a poor fallen woman.

In the next place, our Savior was *aggressive and prompt.* He did not wait for the woman to speak to Him, but He addressed her. "Give me to drink," said He. He did not wait until she had drawn the water from the well, and was about to go, and so give her an excuse for saying, "I cannot be detained, I must get home with the water, and the sun is hot," but no sooner has He seen her and her waterpot than He begins a conversation with His request to her, "Give me to drink." The true soulwinner is like a man who goes out shooting; he is not half asleep, so that when the game presents itself he waits until it has taken wing, and has gone. He is on the alert; if a feather or a leaf moves, he has his gun all ready, and he is prepared for action at once. The cunning fowler spreads his nets early in the morning ere the birds are awake, that when they first begin to move they may be taken in his toils; and the Lord Jesus, with a loving wisdom, went about His work. He began with the woman at once; as soon as she came to the well where He was resting, He spoke to her, and soon led the talk up to the things which concerned the Christ and her own sin, and the way by which the Christ might lift her out of her sin, and make her useful for the conversion of others.

I am afraid that there are some of you who cannot do that; you are so reserved, you say. How often have I told you that the soldier who was so retiring was shot. There was a battle going on, and the man was so modest and retiring that he went into the rear of the fight, and they called him a coward, and shot him dead. I am not going to call you a coward, nor to shoot you; still, I wish you would not get into the rear so much. While souls are perishing it does not do to be reserved and retiring. A man who could swim, and would let his fellowman sink, would hardly be excused if he said, "I was so retiring that I could not push myself upon him. I never had the good man's card, and I did not want to force myself upon him without an introduction, so I let him drown. I was very sorry, but still I never was a pushing person." Are you going to let men be damned? Are you going to let the masses of people in this city perish in their sins? If so, God have mercy upon you! The question will not be, "What will become of London in this case?" but the question will be, "What will become of you, who let men die in their sins without trying to rescue them?" Carry the war into the Enemy's country. Speak to people whom you do not know, whom you have never seen before, as Jesus did. Speak to that woman whom you meet casually and accidentally, as He did; speak to her when the last thing she wants is that you should speak to her. Speak out at once, and let yours be an aggressive Christianity that is prompt to seize every opportunity of doing good. What a model soulwinner, then, have you here!

Next, the Savior was *bold, but He was also wise.* You cannot sufficiently admire the wisdom of our blessed Lord that He spoke to this woman while she was alone. He could not have said to her what He said, and she would never have said to Him what she said, if anybody else had been there. It was necessary that this interview should be held in private. But, oh, you who are so zealous that you are imprudent, you who would fain win souls, but attempt the task without that care which ought to come naturally to every sensible and prudent man, remember that, although Christ spoke alone with this woman, it was in broad daylight, at twelve o'clock, by the well. If some people had been as prudent as the Savior was, they could have afforded to be as zealous as they have been. In the case of such a woman as this, I would have you remember the Savior's wisdom as well as His wondrous condescension. With Nicodemus, the ruler of the Jews, He speaks by night; but with the harlot of Samaria He speaks by day. The soulwinner looks about him, he is wise in his plan of going to work.

There are fish that will only bite in troubled waters, there are some that are not to be taken except at night, and there are others that are only to be caught by daylight. Fit yourself to the case of the person you are seeking to bless. I do not say, be so prudent that you will run no risk; but I will say, be so prudent, especially in certain difficult cases, that you run no unnecessary risk. The Savior could not have selected a better time for talking to such a person; you will see at once that, if even the disciples marveled that He spoke with the woman, it was infinitely wise on His part that it was done at the well-side, and done at noonday. O soulwinner, win souls anyhow! Be willing to risk your own reputation, if necessary, to win them; but it is not necessary, or not usually necessary, and it never should be done except when it is necessary. Your Savior sets you that wise example. Follow Him in this speaking to people singly. I do so much of public preaching that, perhaps, I lose a measure of adaptation for private conversation, yet have I sometimes done the most successful work I have ever done in private rather than in public. Sitting at a table, I have marked a young man who was a stranger to me, and I have asked him to accompany me to the place where I was to preach. I did not know the way, and I asked him to walk with me. A few words on the road won him for Christ, and he has been ever since an earnest upholder of the Gospel, and a very useful one. I do not know whether any were saved by the sermon, but I know that one was converted by the talk on the way there. I know an evangelist who is useful in his public service, but he is also greatly useful to the families in the homes where he stays. Almost in every case, the minister's sons and daughters are converted before he leaves the house, or the servant or a visitor is won by his private conversation. I like that kind of work. Oh, that we all studied this art of speaking to persons one by one! So I say to you again, here is the model soulwinner, copy His example.

Observe how the Savior begins with this woman: "Jesus saith unto her, Give me to drink." When you are fishing, it is not always wise to threw your fly straight at the fish's mouth. Try him a little on one side, and then a little on the other side, and maybe, presently, you will get a bite. So the Savior does not begin by saying to her, "You are a sinful woman." Oh, dear! None but a novice in such a business would start like that. Neither did He begin by saying, "Now, good mistress, I am the Messiah." Well, that was the truth, was it not? Yes, but that was not to come first; He began by saying, "Give me to drink." He must first attract her attention, and influence her mind; then would come the closer work of probing her conscience and changing her heart.

It was only a very ordinary, commonplace request that Jesus made: "Give me to drink." It might have occurred to any one of you to say it, but not to use it as He did. Yet it was a word that was wisely chosen, for it fitted in with the woman's thoughts. She was thinking about drawing water, and Jesus said to her, "Give me to drink." There could be no more suitable metaphor or mode of expression than that of water and drinking, if you are talking to a person who has come to draw water for herself or others to drink.

Besides that, it was an exceedingly significant expression, as full of meaning as an egg is full of meat: "Give me to drink." It contained much within itself. It gave the Savior as wide a field as He could wish for to talk to her about her spiritual thirst, and about that living water which He could put within her, which would abide in her, and be a well, not one to which she would come, but a well that she would carry about with her, and that would be ever springing up within her to everlasting life. So let us learn how to begin wisely with observations that are apparently commonplace, but such as will easily lead to higher things.

I think that the Savior as the model soulwinner is also to be imitated in that *at the very beginning He broke down a barrier.* The Lord Jesus Christ was evidently dressed as a Jew, and this woman came out of Samaria. Now, at once, there was a barrier between the two, for the Jews had no dealings with the Samaritans. Our Lord broke through that caste by saying to her, "Give me to drink." No other expression would do this so well, for to eat and to drink with persons was, after the Oriental fashion, to come into communion with them. "Give me to drink," therefore, shook off from Him all Judaism which would separate Him from this Samaritan. If you are going to try to win people for Christ, always seek to break down everything that would separate. Are you a man of wealth? Well, I do not believe in converting souls by making your diamond rings glitter and flash when you are talking to workingmen. Are you a scientific man? Now, that word of seventeen syllables that you have been so fond of, do not use it, but say something very plain and simple. Or do you happen to belong to any political party? Do not bring that question in; you will not win souls that way, you will be more likely to excite prejudice and opposition. If I were talking to the French, I would devoutly wish I were a Frenchman. If I had to win a German, I should wish to know as much of the idiosyncrasies of that nation as I possibly could. I shall never be ashamed of being an Englishman, but if I could win more souls by being a Dutchman, or a Zulu, I would gladly have any kind of nationality that I might get at the hearts of men. And our Lord Jesus acted just in that spirit when He said to the woman, "Give me to drink." He sank the noble dignity of being a Jew— for, mark you, a Jew is the aristocrat of God—Jesus, even in His humanity, came of a race that is made up of the oldest and noblest of earthly nobility; He dropped that dignity in order that He might talk to this Samaritan woman who was nothing better than a mongrel, for her race was made up of nobody knows what. They pretended to be Jewish when there was anything to get by so doing, and to be Gentile whenever the Jews were in any kind of difficulties. But Jesus did not snub her, nor did He hint that she was in the least degree inferior to Himself. There is no winning souls in any other way than as the Savior won them. God teach us how to win them!

This must suffice for that first point, the model soulwinner.

The Master of Condescension

Now for just a few minutes I want to exhibit our divine Lord and Master in another light; not this time as the model soulwinner, but as the Master of condescension. He seems to me to be so thoughtful, this blessed Lord of ours, the Son of God, the Creator, the first-begotten of God.

He takes his seat there on the well in weariness and thirst; do you not see Him almost ready to faint? What condescension this was, that *He was so destitute that He had not even a draught of water*, or the means to get it. Maker of all springs, Bearer of the key of the rain, Lord of the ocean, and yet He needs water to drink? What a stoop is this, for your Lord and mine to come to this! When He said, "Foxes have holes, and birds of the air have nests; but the Son of man hath not where to lay his head," He had come very low; but now, even the water, which is such a common thing around us that it ripples from the hills, and streams through the vales, even that has fled from Him, and He says, "Give me to drink." Bless your Lord, O you who love Him, kiss His feet, and wonder at His marvelous condescension!

I wonder at His condescension, next, that He not only came into such need, but that *He was so humble as to ask for a drink of water*. He that hears prayer Himself prays. He that listens to the cries of His redeemed, and with the fullness of His majestic bounty opens His hand, and supplies the needs of every living thing, sits there, and says to the woman, "Give me to drink," O Master, how You have impoverished Yourself, how You have humbled yourself, that you should be a beggar of one of Your own creatures, asking for a sip of water!

Admire that condescension still more when you think that He asked it of *her*, of her who had had five husbands, and he with whom she was living was not her husband. Yet Jesus says to her, "Give me to drink." Some of you good women would not have touched her with a pair of tongs, would you? And some of you good men would have passed by her on the other side. Jesus, however, was not only willing to give to her, but He was willing to receive from her; He would put Himself under obligation to a Samaritan sinner. So He says to her, who was not fit to come near Him to unloose the latchets of His shoes—John the Baptist said that he was not worthy to do that, but what was *she* worthy to do?—yet Jesus says even to her, "Give me to drink."

Then notice His condescension again, when she answers Him tartly with a reply that was perhaps civil in tone, but that was virtually a refusal, *He did not upbraid her*. He did not say to her, "Oh, you cruel woman!" No, not a syllable or look of reproof did He give her. He wanted not the water that was in the well, He meant to have her heart, and He did have it, and therefore He went on to speak to her. Is not that a beautiful text, "If any of you lack wisdom, let him ask of God, that giveth to all men liberally, and upbraideth not"? So the Savior will not give this woman a word of upbraiding; she shall be led to upbraid herself, but it shall be for her sin. She shall not be upbraided for her ungenerousness that the Savior has passed over.

This is the crown of Christ's condescension, that He led her not to do what He asked her to do, but *He led her to confess her sin*. He said, "Give me to drink," but, apparently, she did not let down that waterpot, neither did He put it to His lips, parched as they were; but He led her to her confession of sin, her faith in Him, her running to call the men; and all this gave Him meat to eat and water to drink that others knew not of. He had won a soul, and this had refreshed Him after His weariness. We do not hear of His being weary any more, He shook it all off at sight of that sinner saved. He was Himself again, for He had received what He would die to win. He had received a heart returning to the great Father, He had found a soul that trusted in Him.

I wish that I knew how to preach better so that I might lead you to my Master, for I do want you to glorify Him. I have often tried to set Him before you as He hung upon the cross, and as He will come again in His glorious Second Advent; but just now I ask you to adore Him in His weariness as He sits upon the well. He is never lovelier than in His lowliness. There is a grandeur about Him when He rides to battle on His white horse, and summons the hawks and eagles to devour the slain; but we start back from that terrible vision of majesty to the attractiveness of His love when He thus humbles Himself, and makes Himself of no reputation, and talks with a fallen woman. Seeing Him thus condescending, we love, and reverence, and admire, and adore Him; let us do so now.

The Manner of the Working of Grace

I shall have done when I have taken up my third point with considerable brevity, but with no little earnestness. It is this. You have seen the model soulwinner, and the Master of condescension, let us now notice the manner of the working of grace, with the view that we may see it here this evening.

So you have come here, my friend; you have not come to be saved. Oh, no! That is very far from your mind. You came to see the place, you came to look at a building to which a crowd will come and listen to a minister of the Gospel. Yes, yes; but that is no reason why you should not get a blessing; for *this woman only came to draw water*. "There cometh a woman of Samaria to draw water." She had no desire to see Jesus, or to learn of Him; she was only looking for water. Saul went to seek his father's asses, and found a kingdom; so you may find what you never sought, and you may be found of Him whom you never sought. Listen; open your ears. Maybe your day of grace has come, and the great silver bell is striking the hour of your salvation; I hope that it is so. It may be so, though you have no thought of it. You are not converted, you are not a Christian, but you would like to do good in the world, would you not? You desire to do some kindly action, something generous. I have known that thought arise in a great many who yet did not know the Lord. Some people will not ask an unconverted person to give money; I would, for my Master said to a woman who was a great sinner, "Give me to drink." It may be to the ever-lasting good of some of you to do something for the church of God, to do something for the Christ of God; before you know what you are at, it may be that you will commit yourselves by some kindly act. I wish you would do so.

The way to win a person to yourself is not always to do him good, but to let him do you good. Jesus knew that, so He began by saying, "Give me to drink." So sometimes it may be wise—and I would try it now—to say to some of you, "You would like to do someone good, would you not? You would like to do some kindly action." Well, notice, the Master is here tonight, and He has come with much the same cry as He came to the Samaritan woman. *Jesus says to you, "Give me to drink."* "Oh!" say you, "What could I give Christ to drink? If He were here, I would gladly give Him drink. I am sure that, if I were at my cottage door, and He passed by on a dusty day, I would gladly turn the handle of the well, and bring up a bucket of water. Though I am not converted, I would do that." Well dear heart, you may do that; I want you to do it. It is your privilege to refresh the very heart of Christ. If you were not a sinner, you could not do it; but being a guilty sinner, you can do it. Your very guilt and sin give you the possibility of refreshing Him. "How?" you ask. Why, repent of your sin; have done with it, quit it, turn from it. "There is joy in the presence of the angels of God over one sinner that repenteth," It does not say that the angels rejoice, though I believe no doubt that they do; but it is said, "There is joy in the presence of the angels." That is, the angels see the joy of Christ when a sinner repents; they spy it out, and notice it. If you let fall a tear of repentance, if in your heart there is a sense of shame because of your sin, if in your soul there is the resolve to escape from it, you have refreshed Him.

Next, guilty us you are, *you can refresh Him by seeking salvation from Him.* Did He not say to the woman, "If thou knewest the gift of God, and who it is that saith to thee, Give me to drink; thou wouldest have asked of him, and he would have given thee living water"? And when she said to Jesus, "Sir, give me this water," that refreshed Him. Ask this of Him now quietly in your soul. Oh, may God the Holy Spirit persuade you to do so!

Cry to Him to save you; say, "Lord Jesus, save me. I am a young woman, and careless; but save me." "I am a young man, and thoughtless; but save me tonight." By so doing you have given Him to drink, and He is refreshed already. The sweetest draught of all is when you perceive that He is the Christ, and that God has sent Him to save you, and you give yourself up to be saved by Him.

Now trust Him, may the good Spirit lead you now to trust Him! So will you refresh Him; this is the recompense for all His wounds, and even for His death, when sinful souls come and trust Him. I remember hearing of one who, while walking the fields, found a little bird fly into his bosom. He could not understand why the creature should come there, but when he looked up, there was a hawk which had pursued the bird, and the little thing had flown into the bosom of the man for shelter. What think you? Did the man tear it in pieces? Nay, but he kept it safely until he had taken it away from the place where the hawk was, and then he gave it its liberty again. The Lord Jesus Christ will do just that with you if you trust Him. Sin pursues you; fly to His bosom, for there only are you safe. I have heard of a great king who had pitched his royal pavilion, and when he was about to move it, he found that a bird had come, and built its nest there. He was such a king that, although the pavilion was of silk, he ordered his soldiers not to take it down until that bird's young ones were hatched, and could fly. I love the generosity of a prince who will act like that; but my Lord is a nobler and kinder Prince than all others. Oh, what a Prince He is for generosity! Poor bird, if you will dare to trust Him, and make your nest in the pavilion where He dwells, you shall never be destroyed, nor your hope either, but you shall be safe forever!

Oh, that I knew how to bring you to Christ, dear hearers! This is a hot summer's night, and you are weary, perhaps, of my talking; but I would not mind that if I could bring you to Jesus. Oh, that I might have fruit from this sermon also! This week, I believe I might say that I have met and heard of hundreds who, in past years, have been brought to the Savior by the printed sermons. They came to me, grasped my hand, and thanked me, and I praised God; but then I thought, "Yes, God did bless me, and He has blessed the printed sermons, but I want present fruit, and to see sinners now close in with Christ and be eternally saved." Is all that I preach to you only a dream, or a fiction? Then, fling it away from you, and despise both it and me; but if it be true, and if I only tell you of a true salvation, and a true Savior, come and have it, come and trust Him now, for He casts out none who come to Him. May this be the deciding time with many of you, for our Lord Jesus Christ's sake! Amen.

3

How to Become Fishers of Men

And Jesus saith unto them, Follow me, and I will make you fishers of men (Matthew 4:19).

When Christ calls us by His grace we ought not only to remember what we are, but we ought also to *think of what He can make us.* It is, "Follow me, and *I will make you.*" We should repent of what we have been, but rejoice in what we may be. It is not "Follow Me, because of what you are already." It is not, "Follow Me, because you may make something of yourselves," but, "Follow Me, because of what I will make you." Certainly, I might say of each one of us as soon as we are converted, "It does not yet appear what we shall be." It did not seem a likely thing that lowly fishermen would develop into apostles, that men so handy with the net would be quite as much at home in preaching sermons and in instructing converts. One would have said, "How can these things be? You cannot make founders of churches out of peasants of Galilee." That is exactly what Christ did; when we are brought low in the sight of God by a sense of our own unworthiness, we may feel encouraged to follow Jesus because of what He can make us. What said the woman of a sorrowful spirit when she lifted up her song? "He raiseth up the poor out of the dust, and lifteth up the beggar from the dunghill, to set them among princes." We cannot tell what God may make of us in the new creation, since it would have been quite impossible to have foretold what He made of chaos in the old creation. Who could have imagined all the beautiful things that came forth from darkness and disorder by that one fiat, "Let there be light"? And who can tell what lovely displays of everything that is divinely fair may yet appear in a man's formerly dark life when God's grace has said to him, "Let

This sermon was taken from *The Metropolitan Tabernacle Pulpit* and was preached in June of 1886.

there be light"? O you who see in yourselves at present nothing that is desirable, come you and follow Christ for the sake of what He can make out of you. Do you not hear His sweet voice calling to you and saying, "Follow me, and I will make you fishers of men"?

Note, next, that *we are not made all that we shall be*, nor all that we ought to desire to be, when we are ourselves fished for and caught. This is what the grace of God does for us at first, but it is not all. We are like the fishes, making sin to be our element; the good Lord comes, and with the Gospel net He takes us, and He delivers us from the life and love of sin. But He has not wrought for us all that He can do, nor all that we would wish Him to do when He has done this, for it is another and a higher miracle to make us who were fish to become fishers—to make the saved ones saviors—to make the convert into a converter—the receiver of the Gospel into an imparter of that same Gospel to other people. I think I may say to every person whom I am addressing—If you are saved yourself, the work is but half done until you are employed to bring others to Christ. You are as yet but half formed in the image of your Lord. You have not attained to the full development of the Christ-life in you unless you have commenced in some feeble way to tell to others of the grace of God, and I trust that you will find no rest to the sole of your foot until you have been the means of leading many to that blessed Savior who is your confidence and your hope. His word is—Follow Me, not merely that you may be saved, nor even that you may be sanctified, but, "Follow me, and I will make you fishers of men." Be following Christ with that intent and aim, and fear that you are not perfectly following Him unless in some degree He is making use of you to be fishers of men. The fact is that every one of us must take to the business of a man-catcher. If Christ has caught us, we must catch others. If we have been apprehended of Him, we must be His constables, to apprehend rebels for Him. Let us ask Him to give us grace to go afishing, and so to cast our nets that we may take a great multitude of fishes. Oh, that the Holy Spirit may raise up from among us some master fishers, who shall sail their boats in many a sea, and surround great shoals of fish!

My teaching at this time will be very simple, but I hope it will be eminently practical, for my longing is that not one of you that love the Lord may be backward in His service. What says the Song of Solomon concerning certain sheep that come up from the washing? It says, "Every one beareth twins, and none is barren among them." May that be so with all the members of this church, and all the Christian people that hear or read this sermon! The fact is, the day is very dark. The heavens are lowering with heavy thunderclouds. Men little dream of what tempests may soon shake this city, and the whole social fabric of this land, even to a general breaking up of society. So dark may the night become that the stars may seem to fall like blighted fruit from the tree. The times are evil. Now, if never before, every glowworm must show its spark. You with the tiniest farthing candle must take it from under the bushel, and set it on a candlestick. There is need of you all. Lot was a poor creature. He was a very, very wretched kind of believer; but still, he might have been a great blessing to Sodom had he but pleaded for it as he should have done. And poor, poor Christians, as I fear many are, one begins to value every truly converted soul in these evil days, and to pray that each one may glorify the Lord. I pray that every righteous man, vexed as he is with the conversation of the wicked, may be more importunate in prayer than he has ever been, and return to his God, and get more spiritual life, that he may be a blessing to the perishing people around him. I address you, therefore, at this time first of all upon this thought. Oh, that the Spirit of God may make each one of you feel your personal responsibility!

Here is for believers in Christ, in order to their usefulness, *something for them to do*. "Follow me." But, secondly, here is *something to be done by their great Lord and Master*: "Follow me, and I will make you fishers of men." You will not grow into fishers of yourselves, but this is what Jesus will do for you if you will but follow Him. And then, lastly, here is *a good illustration*, used according to our great Master's habit; for scarcely without a parable did He speak to the people. He presents us with an illustration of what Christian men should be—*fishers of men*. We may get some useful hints out of it, and I pray the Holy Spirit to bless them to us.

Something for Believers to Do

First, then, I will take it for granted that every believer here wants to be useful. If he does not, I take leave to question whether he can be a true believer in Christ. Well, then, if you want to be really useful, something for you to do to that end: "*Follow me*, and I will make you fishers of men."

What is the way to become an efficient preacher? "Young man," says one, "go to college." "Young man," says Christ, "*follow Me*, and I will make you a fisher of men." How is a person to be useful? "Attend a training class," says one. Quite right; but there is a surer answer than that——Follow Jesus, and He will make you fishers of men. The great training school for Christian workers has Christ at its head; He is at its head not only as a tutor, but as a leader: we are not only to learn of Him in study, but to follow Him in action. "*Follow me*, and I will make you fishers of men." The direction is very distinct and plain, and I believe that it is exclusive, so that no man can become a fisherman by any other process. This process may appear to be very simple, but assuredly it is most efficient. The Lord Jesus Christ, who knew all about fishing for men, was Himself the dictator of the rule, "Follow Me, if you want to be fishers of men. If you would be useful, keep in My track."

I understand this, first, in this sense: *be separated to Christ.* These men were to leave their pursuits; they were to leave their companions; they were, in fact, to quit the world, that their one business might be, in their Master's name, to be fishers of men. We are not all called to leave our daily business, or to quit our families. That might be rather running away from the fishery than working at it in God's name. But we are called most distinctly to come out from among the ungodly, and to be separate, and not to touch the unclean thing. We cannot be fishers of men if we remain among men in the same element with them. Fish will not be fishers. The sinner will not convert the sinner. The ungodly man will not convert the ungodly man; and, what is more to the point, the worldly Christian will not convert the world. If you are of the world, no doubt the world will love its own; but you cannot save the world. If you are dark, and belong to the kingdom of darkness, you cannot remove the darkness. If you march with the armies of the Wicked One, you cannot defeat them. I believe that one reason why the church of God at this present moment has so little influence over the world is because the world has so much influence over the church. Nowadays we hear Nonconformists pleading that they may do this and they may do that— things which their Puritan forefathers would rather have died at the stake than have tolerated. They plead that they may live like worldlings, and my sad answer to them, when they crave for this liberty, is, "Do it if you dare. It may not do you much hurt, for you are so bad already. Your cravings show how rotten your hearts are. If you have a hungering after such dog's meat, go, dogs, and eat the garbage. Worldly amusements are fit food for mere pretenders and hypocrites. If you were God's children you would loathe the very thought of the world's evil joys, and your question would not be, 'How far may we be like the world?' But your one cry would be, 'How far can we get away from the world? How much can we come out from it?'" Your temptation would be rather to become sternly severe, and ultra-Puritanical in your separation from sin, in such a time as this, than to ask, "How can I make myself like other men, and act as they do?" Brethren, the use of the church in the world is that it should be like salt in the midst of putrefaction; but if the salt has lost its savor, what is the good of it? If it were possible for salt itself to putrefy, it could but be an increase and a heightening of the general putridity. The worst day the world ever saw was when the sons of God were joined with the daughters of men. Then came the flood; for the only barrier against a flood of vengeance on this world is the separation of the saint from the sinner. Your duty as a Christian is to stand fast in your own place and stand out for God, hating even the garment spotted by the flesh, resolving like one of old that, let others do as they will, as for you and your house, you will serve the Lord.

Come, children of God, you must stand out with your Lord outside the camp. Jesus calls to you today, and says, "Follow me." Was Jesus found at the theater? Did He frequent the sports of the race course? Was Jesus seen, think you, in any of the amusements of the Herodian court? Not He. He was "holy, harmless, undefiled, and separate from sinners." In one sense no one mixed with sinners so completely as He did when, like a physician, He went among them healing His patients; but in another sense there was a gulf fixed between the men of the world and the Savior which He never essayed to cross, and which they could not cross to defile Him. The first lesson which the church has to learn is this: Follow Jesus into the separated state, and He will make you fishers of men. Unless you take up your cross and protest against an ungodly world, you cannot hope that the holy Jesus will make you fishers of men.

A second meaning of our text is very obviously this: *abide with Christ,* and then you will be made fishers of men. These disciples whom Christ called were to come and live with Him. They were every day to be associated with Him. They were to hear Him teach publicly the everlasting Gospel, and in addition they were to receive choice explanations in private of the word which He had spoken. They were to be His body-servants and His familiar friends. They were to see His miracles and hear His prayers; and, better still, they were to be with Him, and become one with Him in His holy labor. It was given to them to sit at the table with Him, and even to have their feet washed by Him. Many of them fulfilled that word, "Where thou dwellest I will dwell"; they were with Him in His afflictions and persecutions They witnessed His secret agonies; they saw His many tears; they marked the passion and the compassion of His soul, and thus, after their measure, they caught His Spirit, and so they learned to be fishers of men.

At Jesus' feet we must learn the art and mystery of soulwinning: to live with Christ is the best education for usefulness. It is a great boon to any man to be associated with a Christian minister whose heart is on fire. The best training for a young man is that which the Vaudois pastors were accustomed to give, when each old man had a young man with him who walked with him whenever he went up the mountainside to preach, and lived in the house with him, and marked his prayers and saw his daily piety. This was a fine instruction. Was it not? But it will not compare with that of the apostles who lived with Jesus Himself, and were His daily companions. Matchless was the training of the Twelve. No wonder that they became what they were with such a heavenly tutor to saturate them with His own Spirit! And now today His bodily presence is not among us; but His spiritual power is perhaps more fully known to us than it was to those apostles in those two or three years of the Lord's corporeal presence. There be some of us to whom He is intimately near. We know more about Him than we do about the dearest earthly friend. We have never been able quite to read the friend's heart in all its twistings and windings, but we know the heart of the Well Beloved. We have leaned our heads upon His bosom, and have enjoyed fellowship with Him such as we could not have with any of our own kith and kin. This is the surest method of learning how to do good. Live with Jesus, follow Jesus, and He will make you fishers of men. See how He does the work, and so learn how to do it yourself. A Christian man should be bound apprentice to Jesus to learn the trade of a Savior. We can never save men by offering a redemption, for we have none to present; but we can learn how to save men by warning them to flee from the wrath to come, and setting before them the one great effectual remedy. See how Jesus saves, and you will learn how the thing is done: there is no learning it anyhow else. Live in fellowship with Christ, and there shall be about you an air and a manner as of one who has been made in heart and mind apt to teach, and wise to win souls.

A third meaning, however, must be given to this "Follow me," and it is this: "Obey Me, and then you shall know what to do to save men." We must not talk about our fellowship with Christ, or our being separated from the world to Him, unless we make Him our Master and Lord in everything. Some public teachers are not true at all points to their convictions, and how can they look for a blessing? A Christian man anxious to be useful, ought to be very particular as to every point of obedience to his Master. I have no doubt whatever that God blesses our churches even when they are very faulty, for His mercy endures forever. When there is a measure of error in the teaching, and a measure of mistake in the practice, He may still vouchsafe to use the ministry, for He is very gracious. But a large measure of blessing must necessarily be withheld from all teaching which is knowingly or glaringly faulty. God can set His seal upon the truth that is in it, but He cannot set His seal upon the error that is in it. Out of mistakes about Christian ordinances and other things, especially errors in heart and spirit, there may come evils which we never looked for. Such evils may even now be telling upon the present age, and may work worse mischief upon future generations. If we desire as fishers of men to be largely used of God we must copy our Lord Jesus in everything, and obey Him in every point. Failure in obedience may lead to failure in success. Each one of us, if he would wish to see his child saved, or his Sunday school class blessed, or his congregation converted, must take care that, bearing the vessels of the Lord, he is himself clean. Anything we do that grieves the Spirit of God must take away from us some part of our power for good. The Lord is very gracious and pitiful; but yet He is a jealous God. He is sometimes sternly jealous toward His people who are living in neglects of known duty, or in associations which are not clean in His sight. He will wither their work, weaken their strength, and humble them until at last they say, "My Lord, I will take Your way after all. I will do what You bid me to do, for else You will not accept me." The Lord said to His disciples, "Go ye into all the world, and preach the Gospel to every creature: he that believeth and is baptized shall be saved"; and He promised them that signs should follow, and so they did follow them, and so they will. But we must get back to apostolic practice and to apostolic teaching: we must lay aside the commandments of men and the whimsies of our own brains, and we must do what Christ tells us, as Christ tells us, and because Christ tells us. Definitely and distinctly, we must take the place of servants; and if we will not do that, we cannot expect our Lord to work with us and by us. Let us be determined that, as true as the compass needle is to the pole, so true will we be, as far as our light goes, to the command of our Lord and Master. Jesus says—"Follow me, and I will make you fishers of men." By this teaching He seems to say—"Go beyond Me, or fall back behind Me, and you may cast the net; but it shall be night with you, and that night you shall take nothing. When you shall do as I bid you, you shall cast your net on the right side of the ship, and you shall find."

Again, I think that there is a great lesson in my text to those who preach their own thoughts instead of preaching the thoughts of Christ. These disciples were to follow Christ that they might listen to Him, hear what He had to say, drink in His teaching, and then *go and teach what He had taught them.* Their Lord says, "What I tell you in darkness speak in light: and what you hear in the ear, that preach upon the housetops." If they will be faithful reporters of Christ's message, He will make them "fishers of men." But you know the boastful method nowadays is this: "I am not going to preach this old, old Gospel, this musty Puritan doctrine. I will sit down in my study, and burn the midnight oil, and invent a new theory; then I will come out with my brand-new thought, and blaze away with it." Many are not following Christ, but following themselves, and of them the Lord may well say, "You shall see whose word shall stand, mine or theirs." Others are wickedly prudent, and judge that certain truths which are evidently God's Word had better be kept back. You must not be rough, but must prophesy smooth things. To talk about the punishment of sin, to speak of eternal punishment, why, these are unfashionable doctrines. It may be that they are taught in the Word of God, but they do not suit the genius of the age. We must pare them down. Brothers in Christ, I will have no share in this. Will you? O my soul, come not into their secret! Certain things not taught in the Bible our enlightened age has discovered. Evolution may be clean contrary to the teaching of Genesis, but that does not matter. We are not going to be believers of Scripture, but original thinkers. This is the vainglorious ambition of the period. Mark you, in proportion as the modern theology is preached the vice of this generation increases. To a great degree I attribute the looseness of the age to the laxity of the doctrine preached by its teachers. From the pulpit they have taught the people that sin is a trifle. From the pulpit these traitors to God and to His Christ have taught the people that there is no hell to be feared. A little, little hell, perhaps, there may be; but just punishment for sin is made nothing of. The precious atoning sacrifice of Christ has been derided and misrepresented by those who were pledged to preach it. They have given the people the name of the Gospel, but the Gospel itself has evaporated in their hands. From hundreds of pulpits the Gospel is as clean gone as the dodo from its old haunts; and still the preachers take the position and name of Christ's ministers. Well, and what comes of it? Why, their congregations grow thinner and thinner; and so it must be. Jesus says, "Follow *me*, I will make you fishers of men"; but if you go in your own way, with your own net, you will make nothing of it, and the Lord promises you no help in it. The Lord's directions make Himself our leader and example. It is, "Follow *Me*, follow *Me*. Preach *My* Gospel. Preach what I preached. Teach what I taught, and keep to that." With that blessed servility which becomes one whose ambition it is to be a copyist, and never to be an original, copy Christ even in jots and tittles. Do this, and He will make you fishers of men; if you do not do this, you shall fish in vain.

I close this head of discourse by saying that we shall not be fishers of men unless we follow Christ in one other respect, and that is by endeavoring in all points to *imitate His holiness*. Holiness is the most real power that can be possessed by men or women. We may preach orthodoxy, but we must also live orthodoxy. God forbid that we should preach anything else; but it will be all in vain, unless there is a life at the back of the testimony. An unholy preacher may even render truth contemptible. In proportion as any of us draw back from a living and zealous sanctification we shall draw back from the place of power. Our power lies in this word, "Follow me." Be Jesus-like. In all things endeavor to think, and speak, and act as Jesus did, and He will make you fishers of men. This will require self-denial. We must daily take up the cross. This may require willingness to give up our reputations—readiness to be thought fools, idiots, and the like, as men are apt to call those who are keeping close to their Master. There must be the cheerful resigning of everything that looks like honor and personal glory, in order that we may be wholly Christ's, and glorify His name. We must live His life and be ready to die His death, if need be. O brothers, sisters, if we do this and follow Jesus, putting our feet into the footprints of His pierced feet, He will make us fishers of men. If it should so please Him that we should even die without having gathered many souls to the cross, we shall speak from our graves. In some way or other the Lord will make a holy life to be an influential life. It is not possible that a life which can be described as a following of Christ should be an unsuccessful one in the sight of the Most High. "Follow me," and there is an "I will" such as God can never draw back from: "Follow me, and I will make you fishers of men."

Thus much on the first point. There is something for us to do: we are graciously called to follow Jesus. Holy Spirit, lead us to do it.

Something for the Lord to Do

But secondly, and briefly, there is something for the Lord to do. When His dear servants are following Him, He says, "I will make you fishers of men"; and be it never forgotten that *it is He that makes us follow Him*; so that if the following of Him be the step to being made a fisher of men, yet this He gives us. 'Tis all of His Spirit. I have talked about catching His Spirit, and abiding in Him, and obeying Him, and hearkening to Him, and copying Him; but none of these things are we capable of apart from His working them all in us. "From me is thy fruit found," is a text which we must not for a moment forget. So, then, if we do follow Him, it is He that makes us follow Him; and so He makes us fishers of men.

But, further, if we follow Christ He will make us fishers of men by all our experience. I am sure that the man who is really consecrated to bless others will be helped in this by all that he feels, especially by his afflictions. I often feel very grateful to God that I have undergone fearful depression of spirits. I know the borders of despair, and the horrible brink of that gulf of darkness into which my feet have almost gone; but hundreds of times I have been able to give a helpful grip to brethren and sisters who have come into that same condition, which grip I could never have given if I had not known their deep despondency. So I believe that the darkest and most dreadful experience of a child of God will help him to be a fisher of men if he will but follow Christ. Keep close to your Lord and He will make every step a blessing to you. If God in providence should make you rich, He will fit you to speak to those ignorant and wicked rich who so much abound in this city, and who so often are the cause of its worst sin. And if the Lord is pleased to let you be very poor you can go down and talk to those wicked and ignorant poor people who so often are the cause of sin in this city, and who so greatly need the Gospel. The winds of Providence will waft you where you can fish for men. The wheels of Providence are full of eyes, and all those eyes will look this way to help us to be winners of souls. You will often be surprised to find how God has been in a house that you visit: before you get there, His hand has been at work in its chambers. When you wish to speak to some particular individual, God's providence has been dealing with that individual to make him ready for just that word which you could say, but which nobody else but you could say. Oh, be you following Christ, and you will find that He will, by every experience through which you are passing, make you fishers of men.

Further than that, if you will follow Him He will make you fishers of men *by distinct monitions in your own heart*. There are many monitions from God's Spirit which are not noticed by Christians when they are in a callous condition; but when the heart is right with God and living in communion with God, we feel sacred sensitiveness, so that we do not need the Lord to shout, but His faintest whisper is heard. Nay, He need not even whisper. "You shall guide me with Your eye." Oh, how many mulish Christians there are who must be held in with bit and bridle, and receive a cut of the whip every now and then! But the Christian who follows his Lord shall be tenderly guided. I do not say that the Spirit of God will say to you, "Go and join yourself unto this chariot," or that you will hear a word in your ear; but yet in your soul, as distinctly as the Spirit said to Philip, "Go and join yourself to this chariot," you shall hear the Lord's will. As soon as you see an individual, the thought shall cross your mind, "Go and speak to that person." Every opportunity of usefulness shall be a call to you. If you are ready, the door shall open before you, and you shall hear a voice behind you saying, "This is the way; walk in it," If you have the grace to run in the right way you shall never be long without an intimation as to what the right way is. That right way shall lead you to river or sea, where you can cast your net, and be a fisher of men.

Then, too, I believe that the Lord meant by this that *He would give His followers the Holy Spirit.* They were to follow Him and then, when they had seen Him ascend into the holy place of the Most High, they were to tarry at Jerusalem for a little while, and the Spirit would come upon them and clothe them with a mysterious power. This word was spoken to Peter and Andrew; and you know how it was fulfilled to Peter. What a host of fish he brought to land the first time he cast the net in the power of the Holy Spirit! "Follow me, and I will make you fishers of men."

Brethren, we have no conception of what God could do by this company of believers gathered in the Tabernacle tonight. If now we were to be filled with the Holy Spirit there are enough of us to evangelize London. There are enough here to be the means of the salvation of the world. God saves not by many nor by few. Let us seek a benediction; and if we seek it let us hear this directing voice, "Follow me, and I will make you fishers of men." You men and women that sit before me, you are by the shore of a great sea of human life swarming with the souls of men. You live in the midst of millions; but if you will follow Jesus, and be faithful to Him, and true to Him, and do what He bids you, He will make you fishers of men. Do not say, "Who shall save this city?" The weakest shall be strong enough. Gideon's barley cake shall smite the tent, and make it lay along. Samson, with the jawbone taken up from the earth where it was lying bleaching in the sun, shall smite the Philistines. Fear not, neither be dismayed. Let your responsibilities drive you closer to your Master. Let horror of prevailing sin make you look into His dear face who long ago wept over Jerusalem, and now weeps over London. Clasp Him, and never let go your hold. By the strong and mighty impulses of the divine life within you, quickened and brought to maturity by the Spirit of God, learn this lesson from your Lord's own mouth: "Follow me, and I will make you fishers of men." You are not fit for it, but He will make you fit. You cannot do it of yourselves, but He will make you do it. You do but know how to spread nets and draw shoals of fish to shore, but He will teach you. Only follow Him, and He will make you fishers of men.

I wish that I could somehow say this as with a voice of thunder, that the whole church of God might hear it. I wish I could write it in stars athwart the sky, "Jesus saith, Follow me, and I will make you fishers of men." If you forget the precept, the promise shall never be yours. If you follow some other track, or imitate some other leader, you shall fish in vain. God grant us to believe fully that Jesus can do great things in us, and then do great things by us for the good of our fellows!

A Figure Full of Instruction

The last point you might work out in full for yourselves in your private meditations with much profit. We have here a figure full of instruction. I will give you but two or three thoughts which you can use. "I will make you *fishers of men.*" You have been fishers of fish: if you follow Me, I will make you fishers of men.

A fisher is a person who is *very dependent, and needs to be trustful.* He cannot see the fish. One who fishes in the sea must go and cast in the net, as it were, at a peradventure. Fishing is an act of faith. I have often seen in the Mediterranean men go with their boats and enclose acres of sea with vast nets; and yet, when they have drawn the nets to shore, they have not had as much result as I could put in my hand. A few wretched silvery nothings have made up the whole take. Yet they have gone again and cast the great net several times a day, hopefully expecting something to come of it. Nobody is so dependent upon God as the minister of God. Oh, this fishing from the Tabernacle pulpit! What a work of faith! I cannot tell that a soul will be brought to God by it. I cannot judge whether my sermon will be suitable to the persons who are here, except that I do believe that God will guide me in the casting of the net. I expect Him to work salvation, and I depend upon Him for it. I love this complete dependence, and if I could be offered a certain amount of preaching power by which I could save sinners, which should be entirely at my own disposal, I would beg the Lord not to let me have it, for it is far more delightful to be entirely dependent upon Him at all times. It is good to be a fool when Christ is made to you wisdom. It is a blessed thing to be weak if Christ becomes more fully your strength. Go to work, you who would be fishers of men, and yet feel your insufficiency. You that have no strength, attempt this divine work. Your Master's strength will be seen when your own has all gone. A fisherman is a dependent person, he must look up for success every time he puts the net down; but still he is a trustful person, and therefore he casts in the net joyfully.

A fisherman who gets his living by it is *a diligent and persevering man.* The fishers are up at dawn. At daybreak our fishermen off the Dogger-bank are fishing, and they continue fishing until late in the afternoon. As long as hands can work men will fish. May the Lord Jesus make us hard-working, persevering, unwearied fishers of men! "In the morning sow thy seed, and in the evening withhold not thine hand; for thou knowest not whether shall prosper, either this or that."

The fisherman in his own craft is *intelligent and watchful*. It looks very easy, I dare say, to be a fisherman, but you would find that it was no child's play if you were to take a real part in it. There is an art in it, from the mending of the net right on to the pulling it to shore. How diligent the fisherman is to prevent the fish leaping out of the net! I heard a great noise one night in the sea, as if some huge drum were being beaten by a giant; and I looked out, and I saw that the fishermen of Mentone were beating the water to drive the fish into the net, or to keep them from leaping out when they had once encompassed them with it. Ah, yes! and you and I will often have to be watching the corners of the Gospel net lest sinners who are almost caught should make their escape. They are very crafty, these fish, and they use this craftiness in endeavoring to avoid salvation. We shall have to be always at our business, and to exercise all our wits, and more than our own wits, if we are to be successful fishers of men.

The fisherman is *a very laborious person*. It is not at all an easy calling. He does not sit in an armchair and catch fish. He has to go out in rough weathers. If he that regards the clouds will not sow, I am sure that he that regards the clouds will never fish. If we never do any work for Christ except when we feel up to the mark, we shall not do much. If we feel that we will not pray because we cannot pray, we shall never pray; and if we say, "I will not preach today because I do not feel that I could preach," we shall never preach any preaching that is worth the preaching. We must be always at it, until we wear ourselves out, throwing the whole soul into the work in all weathers, for Christ's sake.

The fisherman is *a daring man*. He tempts the boisterous sea. A little brine in his face does not hurt him; he has been wet through a thousand times, it is nothing to him. He never expected when he became a deep-sea fisherman that he was going to sleep in the lap of ease. So the true minister of Christ who fishes for souls will never mind a little risk. He will be bound to do or say many a thing that is very unpopular, and some Christian people may ever judge his utterances to be too severe. He must do and say that which is for the good of souls. It is not his to entertain a question as to what others will think of his doctrine, or of him; but in the name of the Almighty God he must feel, "If the sea roar and the fullness thereof, still at my Master's command I will let down the net."

Now, in the last place, the man whom Christ makes a fisher of men *is successful*. "But," says one, "I have always heard that Christ's ministers are to be faithful, but that they cannot be sure of being successful." Yes, I have

heard that saying, and one way I know it is true, but another way I have my
doubts about it. He that is faithful is, in God's way and in God's judgment,
successful, more or less. For instance, here is a brother who says that he is
faithful. Of course, I must believe him, yet I never heard of a sinner being
saved under him. Indeed, I should think that the safest place for a person
to be in if he did not want to be saved would be under this gentleman's
ministry, because he does not preach anything that is likely to arouse,
impress, or convince anybody. This brother is "faithful": so he says. Well,
if any person in the world said to you, "I am a fisherman, but I have never
caught anything," you would wonder how he could be called a fisherman.
A farmer who never grew any wheat, or any other crop—is he a farmer?
When Jesus Christ says, "Follow me, and I will make you fishers of men,"
He means that you shall really catch men—that you really shall save some;
for he that never did get any fish is not a fisherman. He that never saved
a sinner after years of work is not a minister of Christ. If the result of his
lifework is *nil*, he made a mistake when he undertook it. Go with the fire
of God in your hand and sing it among the stubble, and the stubble will
burn. Be sure of that. Go and scatter the good seed: it may not all fall in
fruitful places, but some of it will. Be sure of that. Do but shine, and some
eye or other will be lightened thereby. You must, you shall succeed. But
remember this is the Lord's word—"Follow me, and I will make you fishers
of men." Keep close to Jesus, and do as Jesus did, in His Spirit, and He will
make you fishers of men.

Perhaps I speak to an attentive hearer who is not converted at all.
Friend, I have the same thing to say to you. You also may follow Christ,
and then He can use you, even you. I do not know but that He has brought
you to this place that you may be saved, and that in after years He may
make you speak for His name and glory. Remember how He called Saul
of Tarsus, and made him the apostle of the Gentiles. Reclaimed poachers
make the best gamekeepers; and saved sinners make the ablest preachers.
Oh, that you would run away from your old master tonight, without giving him a minute's notice; for if you give him any notice, he will hold you.
Hasten to Jesus, and say, "Here is a poor runaway slave! My Lord, I bear
the fetters still upon my wrists. Will you set me free, and make me your
own?" Remember, it is written, "Him that cometh to me I will in no wise
cast out." Never runaway slave came to Christ in the middle of the night
without His taking him in; and He never gave one up to his old master. If
Jesus make you free you shall be free indeed. Flee away to Jesus, then, on
a sudden. May His good Spirit help you, and He will by and by make you
a winner of others to His praise! God bless you. Amen.

4

How Hearts Are Softened

And I will pour upon the house of David, and upon the inhabitants of Jerusalem, the spirit of grace and of supplications: and they shall look upon me whom they have pierced, and they shall mourn for him, as one mourneth for his only son, and shall be in bitterness for him, as one that is in bitterness for his firstborn. In that day shall there be a great mourning in Jerusalem, as the mourning of Hadadrimmon in the valley of Megiddon (Zechariah 12:10–11).

Hardness of heart is a great and grievous evil. It exists not only in the outside world, but in many who frequent the courts of the Lord's house. Beneath the robes of religion many carry hearts of stone. It is more than possible to come to baptism and the sacred supper, to come constantly to the hearing of the Word, and even, as a matter of form, to attend to private religious duties, and yet still to have an unrenewed heart, a heart within which no spiritual life palpitates, and no spiritual feeling exists. Nothing good can come out of a stony heart; it is barren as a rock. To be unfeeling is to be unfruitful. Prayer without desire, praise without emotion, preaching without earnestness—what are all these? Like the marble images of life, they are cold and dead. Insensibility is a deadly sign. Frequently it is the next stage to destruction. Pharaoh's hard heart was a prophecy that his pride would meet a terrible overthrow. The hammer of vengeance is not far off when the heart becomes harder than an adamant stone.

Many and great are the advantages connected with softness of spirit. Tenderness of heart is one of the marks of a gracious person. Spiritual sensibility puts life and feeling into all Christian duties. He that prays feelingly, prays indeed; he that praises God with humble gratitude, praises Him most acceptably, and he that preaches with a loving heart has the essentials of

---

This sermon was taken from *The Metropolitan Tabernacle Pulpit* and was preached on Sunday morning, September 18, 1887.

true eloquence. An inward, living tenderness, which trembles at God's Word, is of great price in the sight of God.

You are in this matter agreed with me: at least, I know that some of you are thoroughly thus minded, for you are longing to be made tender and contrite. Certain of you who are truly softened by divine grace are very prone to accuse yourselves of being stony-hearted. We are poor judges of our own condition, and in this matter many make mistakes. Mark this: the man who grieves because he does not grieve is often the man who grieves most. He that feels that he does not feel is probably the most feeling man of us all; I suspect that hardness is almost gone when it is mourned over. He who can feel his insensibility is not insensible. Those who mourn that their hearts are hearts of stone, if they were to look calmly at the matter might perceive that they are not all stone, or else there would not be mourning because of hardness. But, whether this be so or not, I address myself to all of you whose prayer is for godly sorrow for sin. It is written in the covenant of grace, "I will take away the stony heart out of your flesh, and I will give you a heart of flesh." I pray that this may be fulfilled in you even now. The object of this sermon is to show how this tenderness is to be obtained, and how an evangelical sorrow for sin can be produced in the heart, and maintained there. I would set forth the simple method by which the inward nature can be made living, feeling, and tender, full of warm emotions, fervent breathings, and intense affections toward the Lord Jesus Christ. While I speak I beseech you to pray: Create in me a tender heart, O Lord, and renew within me a contrite spirit.

It will be instructive to keep to the words of the text. This passage is peculiarly suited to our purpose, and it will add authority to that which we teach. Observe that holy tenderness *arises out of a divine operation.* "I will pour upon the house of David, and upon the inhabitants of Jerusalem, the spirit of grace and of supplications." Secondly, *it is actually wrought by the look of faith*: "And they shall look upon me whom they have pierced, and they shall mourn for him." And, thirdly, the tenderness which comes in this way *leads to mourning for sin of an intense kind*: "They shall mourn for him, as one mourneth for his only son, and shall be in bitterness for him, as one that is in bitterness for his firstborn. In that day shall there be a great mourning in Jerusalem, as the mourning of Hadadrimmon in the valley of Megiddon."

The Holy Tenderness Which Makes Men Mourn for Sin Arises Out of a Divine Operation

First, note that the holy tenderness which makes men mourn for sin arises out of a divine operation. It is not in fallen man to renew his own heart. Can the adamant turn itself to wax, or the granite soften itself to clay? Only He that stretches out the heavens and lays the foundation of the earth can form and reform the spirit of man within him. The power to make the rock of our nature flow with rivers of repentance is not in the rock itself

The power lies in the omnipotent Spirit of God, and it is an omen for good that He delights to exercise this power. The Spirit of God is prompt to give life and feeling. He moved of old upon the face of the waters, and by His power order came out of confusion. That same Spirit at this time broods over our souls, and reduces the chaos of our natural state to light and life and obedience. There lies the hope of our ruined nature. Jehovah who made us can make us over again. Our case is not beyond His power. Is anything too hard for the Lord? Is the Spirit of the Lord limited? He can change the nether millstone into a mass of feeling, and dissolve the northern iron and the steel into a flood of tears. When He deals with the human mind by His secret and mysterious operations, He fills it with new life, perception, and emotion. "God maketh my heart soft," said Job, and in the best sense this is true. The Holy Spirit makes us like wax, and we become impressible to His sacred seal. Remember, you that are hard of heart, that your hope lies this way: God Himself, who melts the icebergs of the northern sea, must make your soul to yield up its hardness in the presence of His love. Nothing short of the work of God within you can effect this. "Ye must be born again," and that new birth must be from above. The Spirit of God must work regeneration in you. He is able of these stones to raise up children to Abraham; but until He works you are dead and insensible. Even now I perceive the goings forth of His power: He is moving you to desire His divine working, and in that gracious desire the work has already begun.

Note next, that as this tenderness comes of the Spirit of God, so *it also comes by His working in full cooperation with the Father and with the Son.* In our text we have all the three persons of the divine Trinity. We hear the Father say, "I will pour upon the house of David the spirit of grace," and that Spirit when poured out leads men to look to Him whom they pierced, even to the incarnate Son of God. Thus the Holy Spirit proceeding from the Father and the Son, fulfills the purpose of the Father by revealing the Son, and thus the heart of man is reached. The divine Father sends forth the Holy Spirit, and He bears witness to the Son of God, and so men come to mourn for sin. We believe in the three persons of the blessed God, and yet we are equally clear that God is one. We see the divers operations of the three divine persons, but we perceive that they are all of one, and work to the self-same end, namely, that grace may reign by delivering us from our natural impenitence, and by causing us to sorrow because we have sinned. The Holy Spirit works not without the Father and the Son, but proves Himself to be in full union with both by His operations upon the soul of man. Do not think, therefore, when you feel the Holy Spirit melting you, that the Father will refuse you: it is He that sent the Holy Spirit to deal with you. Imagine not that you can feel repentance for sin and bow in sorrow at the Savior's feet, and that Jesus will reject you; for it is He who sent the Spirit of grace to bring you to repentance, and make you mourn because of the ill which you have done. The glorious one God, who made the heavens and the earth, is dealing with your heart if the Holy Spirit is now working in you as "the spirit of grace and of supplications."

This operation is an unseen, secret work. You cannot perceive the work of the Spirit by the senses of the flesh; it is spiritually discerned. When the Spirit of God was poured out at Pentecost, there were divers signs attendant thereupon, such as rushing mighty wind, and cloven tongues as it were of fire; but these were outward signs only, the Spirit Himself is inward and secret. The Spirit is as the wind, invisible save by its effects. The Holy Spirit comes as the dew which in soft silence refreshes the tender herb. Not with sound of trumpet or observation of man does the Spirit perform His gracious deeds. His working is one of the secrets and mysteries which no man can explain to his fellow. He that feels the movement of the Holy Spirit knows that a singular work is going on within him, but what it is, or who it is that works it, he knows not. Do not, therefore, expect to be informed when the Spirit is upon you. Marvel not if it should so happen that He is dealing with you now, though you know it not, "For God speaketh once, yea twice, yet man perceiveth it not." The operations of the Holy Spirit are consciously perceived by the human heart, but they are not always attributed to their right cause. Many a man, to use the words of our hymn,

> Wonders to feel his own hardness depart.

He does not know how his new tenderness has been produced. He finds himself anxious to hear and understand the Gospel, and he feels that the Gospel affects him as it never did before, but he does not perceive those "invisible" cords of love which are drawing him toward his Savior. Before long he will cry, "This is the finger of God"; but as yet he perceives not the divine cause. It is well set forth by Mr. Bunyan in his parable of the fire which burned though a man tried to quench it. There was one behind the wall who secretly poured oil upon the fire. He himself was unperceived, but the fire burned because of what he poured on it. You can see the flame, but you cannot see the hidden One who ministers the fuel. The Spirit of God may work in you, my dear hearer, this morning, but it will not be with special token of marvel, or voice, or vision. Not with earthquake, nor wind, nor fire will He come, but with "a still small voice." He may deal with many of you at once, and yet none may see it in his fellow. I expect that He will work upon many at this time, for much prayer has been put up that the Lord Jesus may be glorified in our midst.

But the secret operation of the Spirit is known by its effects, for *it is sweetly productive*. We read in the text of "the spirit of grace and of supplications," which must mean that the Spirit produces graciousness and prayerfulness in the soul upon which He works. The man is now willing to receive the grace, or free favor, of God; he ceases to be proud, and becomes gracious. He is put into a condition in which God's grace can deal with him. As long as you are self-righteous, God cannot deal with you in the way of favor; you are upon wrong ground, for you are making claims which He cannot possibly allow. Mercy and merit can no more blend than fire and water. You must be willing to receive as a free favor what God will never give you if you claim it by right. When you are made conscious of sin, then forgiveness can be granted. When you are malleable under the hammer of God's Word, then will He work His work of love upon you. When you lay your own righteousness aside, and take up the cry, "God be merciful to me a sinner," then shall you go to your house justified. It needs the Spirit of grace to give us grace to receive grace. We are so graceless that we will not even accept grace until God gives us "grace for grace"—grace to accept grace. Blessed is the hour when the Spirit of God comes to us as the Spirit of grace, and works in us that graciousness which makes us value and seek after the free grace of God in its further forms. Grace itself clears out a space in the heart for grace to enter and carry on its work.

It is also said that the Lord will pour out "the spirit of supplications." This is the creation of desires and longings which express themselves in prayer. When the Holy Spirit works savingly upon the heart, then the man begins to approach the mercy seat with frequent and fervent supplications. The words may be broken and confused; but what are words? Sighs, tears, heavings of the breast, and upward glancings of the eye—these are true prayers, and are very prevalent with God. Brethren, we poor preachers cannot make men pray. We can produce a Book of Common Prayer, and read it to them, and ask them to utter the responses; but we cannot make them pray by this means: the Spirit of God is still needed. The child may be taught a form of prayer at its mother's knee, and he may repeat it daily until he is old, and yet he may never have prayed in all those years. Only the Spirit of God can produce the smallest atom of prayer. I tell you, there was never a prayer on earth that God could accept, but what first came down from heaven by the operation of the Spirit of God upon the soul. But here is the point: have you this "spirit of supplications" this morning? Are you groaning, crying, sighing—"Lord, save, or I perish; give me Christ, or else I die"? Well then, I trust you have come under the sacred outpouring promised in the text—"I will pour upon the house of David, and upon the inhabitants of Jerusalem, the spirit of grace and of supplications."

All this leads on toward the tenderness which begets mourning for sin. Again, I say, this is the point from which help must come for the sinner. You that have been striving to feel, and yet cannot feel, and do not feel— you should look to the strong for strength, and to the living for life. He who in the day of His creation breathed into the nostrils of man the breath of life, so that he became a living soul, can infuse the new life into you, and give you with it all the feeling which is natural thereto. Think much of the Holy Spirit, for He can make you live in the truest sense. It is God's to give you a tender heart, not yours to create it within yourself. Do not attempt first to renew your heart, and then to come to Christ for salvation; for this renewal of heart is salvation. Come as you are, confessing all your hardness, your wicked, willful obduracy and obstinacy, confess it all; and then put yourself into the hands of the Spirit, who can remove your hardness at the same time that grace removes your guilt. The Holy Spirit can make your heart as tender as the apple of the eye, and cause your conscience to be as sensitive as a raw wound, which feels the slightest touch. God grant us grace to deal with Him about these things, and not to be looking to ourselves. As well hope to extract juice from the stones of the sea beach, as spiritual feeling from the carnal mind. He who can make the dry bones live, and He alone, can make the hardened mourn over sin.

This Tenderness of Heart and Mourning for Sin Is Actually Wrought by a Faith-Look at the Pierced Son of God

But now I come to the core and center of our subject: This tenderness of heart and mourning for sin is actually wrought by a faith-look at the pierced Son of God. True sorrow for sin comes not without the Spirit of God; but even the Spirit of God Himself does not work it except by leading us to look to Jesus the crucified. There is no true mourning for sin until the eye has seen Christ. It is a beautiful remark of an old divine, that eyes are made for two things at least: first, to look with, and next, to weep with. The eye which looks to the pierced One is the eye which weeps for Him. O soul, when you come to look where all eyes should look, even to Him who was pierced, then your eyes begin to weep for that for which all eyes should weep, even the sin which slew your Savior! There is no saving repentance except within sight of the cross. That repentance of sin which omits Christ is a repentance which will have to be repented of. If such sorrow may be called repentance at all, it is only as wild grapes are yet called grapes, though they have in them none of the qualities and virtues of the clusters of the true vine. Evangelical repentance is acceptable repentance and that only; and the essence of evangelical repentance is that it looks to Him whom it pierced by its sin. Sorrow for sin without faith in Christ is the hard bone without the marrow: it kills, but never blesses. It is a tempest of the soul with thunder and lightning, but no rain. God save us from remorse! It works death.

Mark you, *wherever the Holy Spirit does really come, He always leads the soul to look to Christ*. Never yet did a man receive the Spirit of God to salvation unless he received Him to the bringing of him to look to Christ and mourn for sin. Faith and repentance are born together, live together,

and thrive together. Let no man put asunder what God has joined
together. No man can repent of sin without believing in Jesus, nor believe
in Jesus without repenting of sin. Look, then, lovingly to Him that bled
upon the cross for you, for in that look you shall find pardon, and receive
softening. How wonderful that all our evils should be remedied by that one
sole prescription, "Look unto me and be ye saved, all the ends of the
earth"! Yet none will look until the Spirit of God inclines them so to do,
and He works on none to their salvation unless they yield to His influences
and turn their eyes to Jesus.

Note well that *this look to the pierced One is peculiarly dear to God*.
Observe the change of the pronoun in the middle of the verse: "They shall
look upon *me* whom they have pierced, and they shall mourn for *him*." The
me and the *him* refer to the same person. I lay no special stress upon this,
and I do not attempt to prove any doctrine from it; but certainly it is
remarkable that when we read this verse with defined views as to the one-
ness of Christ with God, and the union of God and man in one person in
the Lord Jesus, we find the pronouns perfectly correct, and understand why
there should be *me* in one case, and *him* in another. If you adopt any other
theory, then the passage would seem to be a jumble of words. It is instructive to note that the Lord, instead of saying, "They shall look upon him
whom they have pierced," cannot keep Himself in the third person, but
bursts upon the scene in His own individuality. Either you have here the
Father regarding Himself as pierced in His Son, or the Lord Jesus Christ
Himself speaking in the spirit of prophecy of Himself, and personally noting
those looks of faith and penitence which are fixed upon His sacred person.
He has such a delight in those looks of believing sorrow, that He mentions
them as having personally beheld them: "They shall look upon me whom
they have pierced." Nothing pleases Jesus more than the faith-looks of His
people. In every stage of their history the glances of believers' eyes are
very precious to Him. "You have ravished my heart, my sister, my spouse;
you have ravished my heart with one of your eyes," says the Bridegroom
in the heavenly canticle. Surely the first glance of a tearful, penitent eye to
Christ is very dear to Him. He says, "I have seen him and observed him."
Nobody sees our look of faith but He Himself and it is not needful that anyone else should see it: is it not a matter between our own souls and our
Lord? He foresaw that look, and in this verse uttered a prophecy concerning it and He looks back upon it with pleasure, keeping it before His
mind as a part of His satisfaction for the travail of His soul. The looks of
faith and the tears of repentance are precious jewels to our Lord Jesus. He
rejoices so much when one sinner repents that the angels see His joy. O
dear hearts, if this morning, in those pews, you look to Christ believingly,
accepting Him as God's salvation, then is the promise fulfilled before the
eyes of Him who spoke it, and said, "They shall look on me whom they

have pierced." He will be glad of your faith: He invites it, He accepts it, He rewards it. "They looked unto him and were lightened: and their faces were not ashamed." Looking to Jesus we receive joy, and we give Him joy. As He delights in mercy, so He delights in those who come to Him and accept His mercy. He was lifted on a cross to be looked at, He was nailed there that He might be a perpetual spectacle, and His heart was pierced that we might see the blood and water, which are our double cure.

The look which blesses us so as to produce tenderness of heart, is a look to Jesus as the pierced One. On this I want to dwell for a season. It is not looking to Jesus as God only which affects the heart, but looking to this same Lord and God as crucified for us. We see the Lord pierced, and then the piercing of our own hearts begins. When the Lord reveals Jesus to us, we begin to have our sins revealed. We see who it was that was pierced, and this deeply stirs our sorrow. Come, dear souls, let us go together to the cross for a little while, and *note who it was* that there received the spear-thrust of the Roman soldier. Look at His side, and mark that fearful gash which has broached His heart, and set the double flood in motion. The centurion said, "Truly this was the Son of God." He who by nature is God over all, "without whom was not anything made that was made," took upon Himself our nature, and became a man like us, save that He was without taint of sin. Being found in fashion as a man, He became obedient to death, even the death of the cross. It is He that died! He who only has immortality condescended to die! He was all glory and power; and yet He died! He was all tenderness and grace, and yet He died! Infinite goodness was hanged upon a tree! Boundless bounty was pierced with a spear! This tragedy exceeds all others! However dark man's ingratitude may seem in other cases, it is blackest here! However horrible his spite against virtue, that spite is cruelest here! Here hell has outdone all its former villainies, crying, "This is the heir; let us kill Him." God dwelt among us, and man would have none of Him. So far as man could pierce his God, and slay his God, he went about to commit the hideous crime; for man slew the Lord Christ, and pierced Him with a spear, and therein showed what he would do with the Eternal One Himself, if he could come at Him. Man is, at heart, a deicide. He would be glad if there were no God: he says in his heart, "No God"; and, if his hand could go as far as his heart, God would not exist another hour. This it is which invests the piercing of our Lord with such intensity of sin: it meant the piercing of God. But why? Why and wherefore is the good God thus persecuted? By the loving kindness of the Lord Jesus, by the glory of His person, and by the perfection of His character, I beseech you be amazed and ashamed that He should be pierced. This is no common death! This murder is no ordinary crime. O man, He that was pierced with the spear was your God! On the cross behold your Maker, your Benefactor, your best Friend!

> Alas! and did my Savior bleed?
> And did my Savior die?
> Would he devote that sacred head
> For such a worm as I?

Look steadily at the pierced One, and *note the suffering* which is covered by the word *pierced*. Our Lord suffered greatly and grievously. I cannot in one discourse rehearse the story of His sorrows: the griefs of His life of poverty and persecution; the griefs of Gethsemane, and the bloody sweat; the griefs of His desertion, denial, and betrayal; the griefs of Pilate's hall, and the scourging, and the spitting, and the mockery; the griefs of the cross, with its dishonor and agony. The sufferings of our Lord's body were only the body of His sufferings.

> 'Twas not the insulting voice of scorn
> So deeply wrung His heart;
> The piercing nail, the pointed thorn,
> Caused not the saddest smart:
>
> But every struggling sigh betray'd
> A heavier grief within,
> How on His burden'd soul was laid
> The weight of human sin.

Our Lord was made a curse for us. The penalty for sin, or that which was equivalent thereto, He endured. "He his own self bare our sins in his own body on the tree." "The chastisement of our peace was upon him; and with his stripes we are healed." Brethren, the sufferings of Jesus ought to melt our hearts. I mourn this morning that I do not mourn as I should. I accuse myself of that hardness of heart which I condemn, since I can tell you His story without breaking down. My Lord's griefs are untellable. Behold and see if there was ever sorrow like unto His sorrow! Here we lean over a dread abyss and look down into fathomless gulfs. Now we are upon great waters, where deep calls to deep. If you will steadfastly consider Jesus pierced for our sins, and all that is meant thereby, your hearts must relent. Sooner or later the cross will bring out all the feeling of which you are capable, and give you capacity for more. When the Holy Spirit puts the cross into the heart, the heart is dissolved in tenderness. *Crux in corde*, as the old preachers used to say, this is the source of godly sorrow. The hardness of the heart dies when we see Jesus die in woe so great.

It behooves us further to *note who it was that pierced Him*—"*They* shall look on me whom *they* have pierced"; the "they," in each case, relates to the same persons. We slew the Savior, even we, who look to Him and live. If a man were condemned and put to death, you might inquire who it was that slew him; and you might be told that it was the judge who condemned him; but that would not be all the truth. Another might blame the jury who brought in the verdict of guilty, or the executioner who actually hanged him; but when you go to the root of the matter, you would find that it was the man's crime which was the real blameworthy cause of his death. In the Savior's case sin was the cause of His death. Transgression pierced Him. But whose transgression? Whose? It was not His own, for He knew no sin, neither was guile found in His lips. Pilate said, "I find no fault in this man." Brethren, the Messiah was cut off, but not for Himself. Our sins slew the Savior. He suffered because there was no other way of vindicating the justice of God and allowing us to escape. The sword which else had smitten us was awakened against the Lord's Shepherd, against the Man that was Jehovah's Fellow. Truly may we sing

> 'Twas for my sins my dearest Lord
> Hung on the cursed tree,
> And groan'd away a dying life
> For thee, my soul, for thee.
>
> Oh, how I hate those lusts of mine
> That crucified my God;
> Those sins that pierced and nail'd his flesh
> Fast to the fatal wood!
>
> Oh, if my soul were form'd for woe,
> How would I vent my sighs!
> Repentance should like rivers flow
> From both my streaming eyes.

If this does not break and melt our hearts, let us *note why He came into a position in which He could be pierced by our sins*. It was love, mighty love, nothing else but love which led Him to the cross. No other charge can ever be laid at His door but this, that He was "found guilty of excess of love." He put Himself in the way of piercing because He was resolved to save us. He loved us better than He loved Himself. And shall we hear of this, and think of this, and consider this, and remain unmoved? Are we worse than brutes? Has all that is human quitted our humanity? If God the Holy Spirit is now at work, a sight of Christ will surely melt the heart of stone.

Furthermore, notice that *looking to the pierced One causes mourning in every case*. All hearts yield to this. Under the power of the Holy Spirit *this works efficaciously of itself*. Nothing else is needed. "They shall look upon me," and "they shall mourn." Faith in Christ is sufficient for the production of acceptable and deep repentance; this, and this only, without mortifications and penances.

Let me also say to you, beloved, that *the more you look at Jesus crucified, the more you will mourn for sin*. Growing thought will bring growing tenderness. I would have you look much at the pierced One, that you may hate sin much. Books which set forth the passion of our Lord, and hymns which sing of His cross, have ever been most dear to saintly minds because of their holy influence upon the heart and conscience. Live at Calvary, beloved; for there you will live at your best. Live at Calvary, and love at Calvary, until *live* and *love* become the same thing. I would say, look to the pierced One until your own heart is pierced. An old divine says, "Look at the cross until all that is on the cross is in your heart." He further says: Look at Jesus until He looks at you. Steadily view His suffering person until He seems to turn His head and look at you, as He did at Peter when he went out and wept bitterly. See Jesus until you see yourself: mourn for Him until you mourn for your sin.

The whole of this subject leads me to observe that the conversion of the Jews will come from a sight of the crucified Messiah. I conclude from this text that Israel will be brought to know the Lord, not by a vision of Christ in His glory, but by a sight of Christ in His humiliation. "They shall look upon me whom they have pierced, and shall mourn for him." But I also conclude that this holds good of all mankind. By the preaching of Christ crucified will their hearts be broken. The cross is God's hammer of love, wherewith He smites the hearts of men with irresistible blows. Men tell us we should preach Christ as an example. We do preach Him as an example, and rejoice to do so, but we can never allow that view of our Lord to overshadow our preaching of Him as a sacrifice for sin. He suffered in the room, and place, and stead, of guilty men, and this is the Gospel. Whatever others may preach, "we preach Christ crucified." We will ever bear the cross in the forefront. The substitution of Christ for the sinner is the essence of the Gospel. We do not keep back the doctrine of the Second Advent but, first and foremost, we preach the pierced One for this it is that shall lead to evangelical repentance, when the Spirit of grace is poured out. O brethren, whatever else you preach, or do not preach, preach Christ crucified! Jesus Christ my Lord as crucified is my main topic, and shall be until I die. I trust you feel a pleasure in thinking of the Lord Jesus in any character in which He is revealed, but yet the cross is that whereon He is most lifted up, and this is the chief attraction for sinful men. Though it be to the Jews a stumbling block and to the Greeks foolishness, it is still the power of God for salvation to everyone that believes.

The Sight of Christ Crucified Will Produce a
Mourning for Sin of a Very Thorough Character

My time is nearly over, and therefore I must only for a minute touch upon the surface of my third subject: the sight of Christ crucified will produce a mourning for sin of a very thorough character. It will be immediate. If the Spirit of God grants us an inward sight of Christ, we shall bleed inwardly at once. The sentences are fast joined together—"They shall look upon me whom they have pierced, and they shall mourn." How rapidly the Spirit of God often works! "His word runneth very swiftly." With a single blow of grace the bars of iron are broken. Saul of Tarsus was foaming at the mouth with rage against Jesus of Nazareth and His disciples, but a flash and a word changed him. "Why persecutest thou me?" showed him the pierced Lord, and, "Lord, what wilt thou have me to do?" was his speedy answer. One glimpse at Christ will make yonder stubborn sinner bow the knee. Look on him, Lord!

This mourning, according to our text, is *refined and pure*. They shall mourn *for Him*, they shall be in bitterness *for Him*. For Jesus they sorrow rather than for themselves. Sin is not mentioned in these verses, and yet the sorrow is all concerning sin. The grief for sin itself is overborne and compassed about by the greater grief occasioned by the sad results of sin upon the person of the pierced One. Sin is grieved over as it is against the Lord: even as David cries, "Against thee, thee only, have I sinned." The mourning of a penitent is not because of hell: if there were no hell he would mourn just as much. His grief is not for what sin might cost him, but for what it has cost the Substitute. He bemoans himself thus: "Oh, how could I have pierced Him! How could I have wounded the Beloved? Lover of my soul, how could I have pierced You?" True penitents smite upon their breasts as they behold their Savior bleeding on the tree. This is the sense of sin which is the mark of God's electing love, the token of the effectual calling of His grace.

In this mourning there is *a touching tenderness*: "They shall be in bitterness for him, as one that is in bitterness for his firstborn." It is not a son lamenting for a father, for there the grief might be as much for the loss of the father's care and help as for the father's self; but in the case of a father mourning his young son, the father is not thought to lose anything but his boy; his grief is for the child himself. Mourning for a son is caused by a peculiarly pure and unmixed love. Somewhat that is of the earth, earthy, may enter into the mourning for a wife; but for his son a father laments with a love which none may question. For an only son the mourning is bitter indeed, and for a firstborn it is as gall and wormwood. The Israelite was specially sensitive concerning the death of his offspring. To lose his firstborn was as when a nation loses its prince. To lose his only son was to quench the light of the house. The old man mourns, "I am as good as dead. I am blotted out of the book of the living, for I have now no son to bear my name. The lamp has gone out in my tent, for my son, my only son, my firstborn, has gone down to the gates of the grave!" The case was hopeless for the future; none remained to continue his family among those who sit in the gate, and the old man rent his clothes and wept sore. It is a bitter mourning which we have when we see Jesus slain by our sins. Were it not for the consequences which grace has caused to flow therefrom, our sorrow would be hopeless and helpless; for we feel that in killing Jesus we have destroyed our best, our only hope, our one and only joy. His death was the hiding of the sun, and the shaking of the earth, and we feel it to be so within our own souls. All that is worth having is gone when Jesus is gone. When God's only Son, His firstborn, dies, we sympathize with the great Father, and feel ourselves bereaved of our chief joy, our hope, our delight.

This sorrow is *intense*. The word *bitterness* is used twice. Sorrow at the cross-foot is sorrow indeed, sorrow upon sorrow, grief upon grief. Then we have bitterness and bitterness, bitterness upon bitterness, the bitterness of bitterness. Thank God, it is a healthy tonic: he that has tasted this bitterness may say, "Surely the bitterness of death is past."

And this kind of mourning is *very extraordinary*. The prophet could not recollect any mourning which he had ever heard of that was like it, except the lamentation of the people for the death of Josiah. Then all Judah mourned, and Jeremiah wrote sad dirges, and other prophets and poets poured forth their lamentations. Everywhere throughout the land there went up an exceeding great and bitter cry, for the good king had fallen, and there were no princes of like mind to follow him. Alas, poor nation! it was your last bright hour which saw him ride to the battle; in his death your star has set! In the valley of Hadadrimmon the mourning began, but it spread through all the land. The fatal fight of Megiddon was wailed by every woman in Jerusalem. Bravely had Josiah kept his word, and sought to repel the Egyptian invader; but the hour of Judah's punishment was come, and Josiah died. A mourning as sincere and deep comes to us when we perceive that Jesus died for us. Blessed be His name, the joy that comes of it when we see sin put away by His death turns all the sorrow into joy.

This mourning is *personal grief*; every man repents apart, and every woman apart. It is a private, personal grief; it is not produced by the contagion of example, but by the conviction of the individual conscience. Such sorrow is only to be assuaged by Jesus Christ Himself when He is revealed as the salvation of God.

Brethren, I am conscious that I have not preached as I ought to have preached this morning. I have been mastered by my subject. I could sit down alone and picture my divine Master on the cross. I delight to do so. It is my comfort to meditate on Him. I see Him hanging on the tree, and carefully survey Him, from His head encircled with the thorns, down to His blessed feet, made by the nails to be fountains of crimson blood. I have wept behind the cross at the marks of the dread scourging which He bore; and then coming to the front I have gazed upon His pierced hands, and lingered long before that opened side. Then I feel as if I could die of a pleasing grief and mournful joy. Oh, how I then love and adore! But here before this crowd I am a mere lisper of words—words which fall far below the height of this great argument. Ah me! Ah me! Who among the sons of men could fitly tell you of His unknown agonies, His piercing anguish, His distraction and heartbreak? Who can fully interpret that awful cry of "Eloi, Eloi, lama sabachthani? My God, my God, why hast thou forsaken me?" Alone I can hide my face and bow my head; but here what can I do? O Lord, what can your servant do?

> Words are but air, and tongues but clay,
> And thy compassions are divine.

I cannot tell of love's bleeding, love's agony, love's death! If the Holy Spirit will graciously come at this time, and put me and my words altogether aside, and set my Lord before you, evidently crucified among you, then shall I be content, and you will go home thoughtful, tender, hating sin, and therefore more deeply happy, more serenely glad than ever before. The Lord grant it for His name's sake! Amen.

5

Shame Leading to Salvation

Fill their faces with shame; that they may seek thy name, O Lord
(Psalm 83:16).

This is a very terrible psalm. It contains some prayers against the enemies of God and of His people that crash with the thunder of indignation. You know that we are bidden to love our enemies, but we are never commanded to love God's enemies. We may not hate any men as men; but as they are opposed to God, to truth, to righteousness, to purity, we may, and we must, if we are ourselves right-minded, feel a burning indignation against them. Did you ever read the story of "the middle passage" in the days of the African slave trade, when the Negroes died by hundreds, or were flung into the sea to lighten the ship? Did you ever read of those horrors without praying, "O God, let the thunderbolts of Your wrath fall on the men who can perpetrate such enormities"? When you heard the story of the Bulgarian atrocities, did you not feel that you must, as it were, pluck God's sleeve, and say to Him, "Why does Your justice linger? Let the monsters of iniquity be dealt with by You, O Lord, as they deserve to be"?

Such is the spirit of this psalm. But I like best this particular verse in it because, while it breathes righteous indignation against the wicked, it has mixed with it the tender spirit of love. "Fill their faces with shame," prays the psalmist, but overrule Your severity for their everlasting good, "that they may seek thy name, O Lord." The worst fate that I wish to any hearer of mine who is without God, and without hope in the world, is that this prayer may be prayed by honest and loving hearts for him and for others like him, "Fill their faces with shame; that they may seek thy name, O Lord."

Ungodly Men Have Good Cause to Be Afraid

Let us talk a little, first, of *their wrong to their Master*. If I might take

---

This sermon was taken from *The Metropolitan Tabernacle Pulpit* and was preached on Sunday evening, October 31, 1886.

each one of you by the hand, I would say to you, "Friend, you believe in the existence of God, your Maker, do you not? Well, then, have you treated Him rightly? If you have lived in the world twenty years, or perhaps even forty or fifty years, and yet you have never served Him, do you think that is quite just to Him? If He made you, and has fed you, and kept you in being all these years, has He not a right to expect some service from you? I might go further, and say, has He not a right to expect your love? Does He ask more than He should ask when He says, "Thou shalt love the Lord thy God with all thine heart, and with all thy soul, and with all thy might"? Yet you have lived these many years, and scarcely thought of Him; certainly, you have not spoken to Him, you have never confessed your faults to Him, or sought His forgiveness. To all intents and purposes, you have lived as if there were no God at all. Yet, in your earthly affairs, you are a very honest man, and you pay everybody else his due; why do you, then, rob your God of what is justly His? There is not a man in the world who could say truly of you that you had dealt dishonorably with him. You pride yourself upon your uprightness and integrity; but must God alone, then, be made to suffer through your injustice? Out of all beings, must He alone who made all other beings be the only one to be neglected? He is first of all; do you put Him last? He is best of all; do you treat Him worst? If so, I think that such conduct as this is a thing to be ashamed of, and I pray that you may be heartily ashamed of it.

Let me quit that line of thought, and remind you, next, that there are many ungodly men, and I suppose some here present, who ought to be ashamed because they are acting *in opposition to light and knowledge, contrary to their consciences, and against their better judgments*. There are many unconverted men who can never look back upon any day of their lives without having to accuse themselves of wrong; and although they are not Christians, they would scarcely attempt to justify their position; when they act wrongly, there is a voice within them which tells them that they are doing wrong. They are not blind; they could see if they chose to see. They are not deaf, except that there are none so deaf as those who will not hear. It is a horrible thing for a man to be always holding down his conscience, like a policeman holding down a mad dog. It is a terrible thing for a man to have to be at war with himself in order to destroy himself; his better self resisting, and struggling, as it were, after salvation, but his worse self thrusting back the higher part of his being, stifling his conscience, and drowning the cries of any approach to betterness that may be within him. God forbid that men should act thus, and sin against light and knowledge! I venture very quietly, but very solemnly, to tell any who are doing so that they ought to be ashamed of such conduct, they ought to blush at the very thought of acting thus against such light as they have, and against the convictions of their own conscience.

There are some also of my hearers—I speak very positively upon this point—who ought to be ashamed because of *their postponements of what they know to be right*. They have again and again put off the observance of duties which they know and admit to be incumbent upon them. "I ought to repent of sin," says one; and then he adds, "and I will one of these days." "I ought to be a believer in Christ"—he admits that—"and I shall be, I hope, before I die." Oh, how fairly you talk, Mr. Procrastinator! You know what ought to be done at once, but you leave it all for the future. Do you not know that, every time a man neglects a duty, he commits a sin? That which you admit is your duty causes you, every moment it is delayed, to commit sin by the delay; and by delay obedience becomes more difficult, and you yourself become continually more likely to commit yet greater sin. I do think that a man who says, "I ought to believe in Christ, I ought to repent of sin, I ought to love God," and yet says, "Well, I will do so at a more convenient season," ought to be ashamed of himself for talking and acting in such a wicked fashion; I pray God that he may be.

I shall come more pointedly home to some when I say that they ought to be ashamed because of *their violation of vows which they have made*. You were very ill, a little while ago, and you said, "O God, if You will but spare my life, and restore me to health and strength, I will rise from this bed to be a better man!" God did raise you up, but you are not a better man. You were seriously injured in an accident, and likely to die, and in your distress you prayed, "O God, if You will prolong my unworthy life, I will turn over a new leaf; I will be a very different man in future!" Well, you are a different man, for you are worse than you used to be before the accident; that is all the change that has been wrought in you. God keeps a register of the vows that are so lightly broken here below, but so well remembered up in heaven, and the day will come when they shall be brought out to the condemnation of those who made them, and then failed to keep them. If you are determined to be a liar, lie not to God. If you are resolved to make promises only to break them, at least trifle not with Him in whose hand your life is, and whose are all your ways. He who must play the fool had better do it with some fellow fool, and not parade his folly before "him that rideth upon the heavens by his name JAH." Think then, dear friends, of vows violated, and blush because of them.

Moreover, it seems to me—and I shall leave it to your judgment to consider and approve what I say—that every man ought to be ashamed of not loving the Lord Jesus Christ, and *not trusting such a Savior as the Lord Jesus Christ is*. God in human flesh, bleeding, dying, bearing the penalty of human sin, and then presenting Himself freely as our Sacrifice, and saying that whosoever believeth in Him shall not perish, but shall have everlasting life; do you push Him away from you? Will you trample on His blood, and count it an unholy thing? Will you despise His cross? It sometimes seems to me that blasphemy and adultery and murder—tremendous evils though these be—scarcely reach the height of guilt that comes through refusing the great love of Christ, thrusting Him aside whom God took from His bosom, and gave up to die that men might live through Him. If you must spite anybody, spite anybody but the Christ of God. If you mean to refuse a friend, refuse any friend but the bleeding Savior, who spared not His very life, but poured out the floods from His heart that He might save the guilty.

So, you see, dear friends, that He who loves not Christ, and trusts not Christ, has good cause to be ashamed.

I will not say any more upon this first point, except just one thing; that is, *a man ought to be ashamed who will not even think of these things.* There are great numbers of our fellow citizens in London, and our fellow creatures all the world over, who have resolved not to think about religion at all. There stands the house of God, but in that same street there is hardly one person who ever enters it. There is a Bible in almost every house, but many, nowadays, will not read it, or try to understand it. I would have thought that common and idle curiosity alone might have made men anxious to understand the Christian religion, the way of salvation by a crucified Savior. I should have fancied that they would have strayed in to see what our worship was like; if it had been the worship of Mumbo Jumbo, they would have wanted to see that, but when it is the worship of the Lord God Almighty, and of His Son Jesus Christ, the multitudes seem to be utterly indifferent to it. From the cross I hear my dying Master cry, "Is it nothing to you, all ye that pass by? behold, and see if there be any sorrow like unto my sorrow." Even the voice of His gaping wounds, and the voice of His bloody sweat, and the voice of His broken heart seem to fall upon hearts that will not listen, and upon ears that are as deaf as stones. Many who come to hear the Gospel go their way to their farms and to their merchandise, but they care nothing for Him who is worth more than all beside. O sirs, in that day when this solid earth shall rock and reel, when the heavens being on fire shall be dissolved, when the stars shall fall like the leaves of autumn, and when there shall sail into the sky, conspicuous to the gaze of all, the great white throne, and on it shall sit the despised Redeemer, you will repent then, and regret when it is too late that you gave Him none of your thoughts, but put the affairs of religion wholly on one side! Investigate this matter, I charge you. By what your immortal souls are worth, by an eternal heaven and an endless hell—and there are both of these, despite what some say—I charge you, as I shall meet you at the judgment seat, and would be clear of your blood, do give earnest attention to the things that make for your peace, and consider the claims of God and of His Christ, and seek to find the way of salvation by faith in Jesus.

Thus, surely, I have said enough upon this first point; ungodly men have good cause to be ashamed.

Shame Is a Very Desirable Thing If It Drives Them to God

Now, secondly, concerning these ungodly people, let me show you that shame is a very desirable thing if it drive them to God. Hence the prayer, "Fill their faces with shame, that may seek thy name, O Lord."

I have known shame to drive men to God in various ways. Sometimes, shame attends *the breaking up of self-righteousness.* I know a young fellow who had been a very upright moral man all his days. He seemed to think that he should go to heaven by his good works; but he had no notion of a Savior, and no regard for the things of Christ. One day, being in the workshop, he upset an oil can; the master, a bad-tempered man, inquired sharply who had wasted the oil, and this man, who had always until then been truthful, on this occasion told a lie, and said that he did not upset the can. Nobody found him out, mark you; he was so highly respected that his employer fully believed that he had not done it; but he went down greatly in his own esteem. He said to me, "Sir, my righteousness went all to pieces in a moment. I know that I had told a lie; I felt disgusted with myself, and when I got out of the shop, for the first time in my life I cried to God for mercy, for I saw myself to be a sinner." Now I do not wish any of you to commit further sin in order that you may realize your true condition in God's sight. You have done enough evil already, without doing any more; but I would like some one of these sins to come so sharply home to you, that it would make you feel ashamed, and give up all pretense of self-righteousness, and just come by faith to Christ, and take His righteousness to be your perfect covering before God.

I have known this shame to operate in some, when they have done wrong, and have *lost the repute they enjoyed among their fellow creatures.* They have been found out in doing wrong, and, sad as it was to them, yet when they felt that they could no longer come to the front, and lead as they used to do, when they knew that they must get somewhere in the rear rank, and that, if their true character became known, people would shun them, then it was that, like the prodigal son, they said, "I will arise, and go to my Father." There is many a man who stands high in popular esteem, but who is never likely to be saved, for he is too proud and self-conceited ever to seek the Savior. But there have been some others who, for a grave fault, have had all their glory trailed in the mire, and then they have sought the face of Christ. I scarcely care how or why they do seek that blessed face, so long as they find it, and are saved.

There are two instances, then, in which shame drives men to God: first, when a man has lost his own good opinion of himself, and next, when he has lost the good opinion of others. Filled with shame, he has often fled to Christ.

So have I seen it in the case of *failure driving a man to the Strong for strength.* There is a young man who has come lately from the country; he knew the temptations of London, but he said to his father and mother, "You will never hear of your son John doing such things." Ah, John! they have not heard of it yet, but you have done a great many evil things by now, and you ought to be ashamed. If your father finds it out, as likely enough he will, you will be ashamed; but, seeing that you have found yourself out, I wish that you would be ashamed before the Lord now. O that virtuous John, that excellent youth, that dear young man! You were just going to join the church, were you not? Where were you last night? Ah, not drinking of the communion cup, I will warrant you! Where are you now? O John, if you could have seen yourself, six months ago, to be what you now are, you would not have held your head so high when you came away from your native town! But your failure, that wretched broken back of yours, with which you meant to stand so bolt upright, should all help to drive you to God, your father's God and your mother's God. My dear friend, I pray you seek the face of the Most High, and begin again; for, John, though you cannot stand by yourself, God can make you to stand. With a new heart and a right spirit, you can do a deal better than you have done in the past in your own strength, which is utter weakness. I have known a teetotaler, who has felt himself quite safe because he wore a blue ribbon, to become a drunkard, notwithstanding that very desirable badge. If that is your case, my brother, when you are ashamed of yourself on that account, as well you may be, go to the Lord for a new heart and a right spirit, and then begin again, that you may truly be what you aspire to be, an example to others. So, you see, that shame in such a case of failure as I have described, may bring a man to Christ.

I have also known men brought to Christ with shame of another sort, shame of mental error leading to a humble faith. A young gentleman felt that he had heard the old-fashioned Gospel long enough, and he should like to go and hear the new Gospel. More light is said to have broken out of late; I can only tell you that it comes from some very dark places, and I do not think there is much light in it. But this gentleman thought that he must know about this new light, and he has kept going further and further, and the new light has led him, like the will-o'-the-wisp does, into all sorts of boggy places; and now he begins to feel that he can do a great many things which once he dared not do, until suddenly the thought occurs to him, "Where have I got to now?" He has become an unbeliever altogether; he who was once almost persuaded to be a Christian has run into very wild ways, and nothing is sure with him; it is all rocking to and fro before him, like the waves of the sea, and there is nothing solid left. Ah now you begin to be ashamed, do you? You are not, after all, so full of wisdom as you thought you were. Come back, then; come back, and believe the old Book, and trust the Savior who has brought so many to the eternal kingdom. Believe His words, follow in His track, and this very shame on account of your fancied intellectual prowess, which has turned out to be sheer folly, will bind you in future to the simple cross of Christ, and you will never go away from it again.

I want to suggest one thing more before I leave this part of my subject. In this congregation there must be a good many men and women who might do well to look back upon *the utter uselessness of their past lives*. As I looked along these galleries, at the immense preponderance of men in the congregation, which is so usual with us, I thought, "What a number there must be here who, if they threw the weight of their influence in with us, and sought to do good to others, would be immensely valuable to the church of God!" But are there not many, perhaps even professing Christianity, who, in looking back upon their past lives, will be obliged to say that they have done nothing? What did you ever accomplish, dear friends? There was a lady, who had a large sum of money in her possession, much more than sufficient for her needs; she was a Christian woman, living a quiet, comfortable life by the seaside. One night, as she walked up and down the beach, she said to herself, "What have I ever done for Him who died for me! If I were to die now, would anybody miss me? When my life is finished, shall I have accomplished anything?" She felt that she had done nothing; so she went home, and ruminated upon what she could do. She began to live very hard that she might save all she could, and she accumulated quite a large amount, for she had an object to live for. The orphanage at Stockwell is the outcome of that good woman's thought at the seaside; she consecrated her substance to the starting of a home where boys and girls, whose fathers were dead, might be housed. I cannot but think of her, and then say to myself, "Are there not many ladies, many gentlemen, many men, many women, who might walk up and down, and say, 'Well, now, when I die, who will miss me?'" I believe that there are numbers of people who call themselves Christians, who might be tied hand and foot, and flung into the Atlantic, and nobody would miss them beyond the two or three members of their own families. They do nothing; they are living for nothing. "Oh, but!" they say, "we are accumulating money." Yes, yes; that is like a jackdaw hiding rubbish behind the door, putting away everything he can get. Poor jackdaw! That is what you are doing, nothing more. To get money is well enough, if you get it that you may use it well; and to learn is right enough, if you learn with the view of teaching others. If life is not to be wasted, there must be a living to God with a noble purpose; and they who have lived in vain with multitudes of opportunities of doing good ought to be ashamed; and such shame should bring them to the Savior's feet in humble penitence. God give such shame as that to any here who ought to have it, that they may at once seek the name of the Lord!

The Lord Is Willing Now to Receive Those Who Are Ashamed of Themselves

I must close by speaking only briefly upon the last head of my discourse, which is, the Lord is willing now to receive those who are ashamed of themselves. Let me say that again. The Lord is waiting and willing now to receive to the love of His heart those who are thus ashamed of themselves.

I do not think that I need say much to enforce this great truth. Is there one person here who is ashamed of himself because of his past sin? Then, you are the man I invite to come to that Savior who bore your shame in His own body on the tree. You are the sort of man for whom He died. Remember how He Himself said, "The Son of man is come to seek and to save that which was lost"; and one mark of the lost is their deep sense of shame, when they get to be so ashamed of themselves that they try to hide away from the gaze of their fellow creatures. If you are ashamed of yourself, Christ is willing to receive you; behold, He stands before you with open arms, and bids you come and trust Him, that He may give you rest.

You are the sort of man to come to Christ, because, first, *you have the greatest need of Him.* In the time of famine, we give the meal away first to the most hungry family. He who has alms to distribute to the poor, if he be wise, will give the most speedy relief to those who are the most destitute; and you, my dear hearer, are like that; if you are ashamed of yourself, you are the bankrupt, you are the beggar, you are the sort of sinner whom Jesus came to save. God's elect are known by this mark—in their own natural estate they are as poor as poverty itself. If you are empty, there is a full Christ for you. If your last mite is gone, heaven's treasures are all open for you. Come and take them, take them freely, as freely as you breathe the air, as freely as you would drink of the flowing river. Come and take Christ without question and without delay, take Him now and happy be; and the way to take Him is to trust Him, to trust yourself with Him absolutely. He is a Savior; let Him save you. Have no finger in the work yourself, but leave it all to Him. Commit yourself entirely and absolutely to that mighty hand that molded the heavens and the earth, to that dear hand that was nailed to the tree. Jesus can save you, He will save you, He must save you, He is pledged to save you; if you have believed in Him, He has saved you, and you may go your way, and rejoice with joy unspeakable and full of glory.

Next, if you are ashamed of yourself, you are the man to come Christ, because *you will make no bargains with Him.* You will say, "Save me, Lord, at any price and in any way!" And you are the man who will *give Him all the glory if you are saved.* That is the kind of sinner Jesus loves to save; not one who will run away with the credit of his salvation, and say, "I was always good, and I had many traces of an excellent character about me before Christ saved me." Such a man might try to divide with the Lord the glory of his salvation, so he is not likely to be saved; but God delights to save those in whom there is no trace of goodness, no hope of goodness, no shadow of goodness, the men who not only feel that God may well be ashamed of them, but who are absolutely ashamed of themselves.

In preaching on this important theme, I have not used any grace of diction, nor have I made any display of oratory; but I have plainly told you the Gospel message, and I have expostulated with those of you who have not considered it. I wish that, by the grace of God, even ere this night passes away, you would come and rest yourselves on Christ. The Holy Spirit is here, blessedly working upon some hearts. If He is not yet working upon others of you, I pray that He may now begin to do so. Remember, my dear hearers, that you are all mortal, and some of you may soon be gone from earth. During the past week, I personally have lost some very choice friends who died quite suddenly. There was a young friend who was here a Sabbath or so ago; he was taken ill last Sunday afternoon, and he was gone in a few hours. His sorrowing friends are absent today, for he was laid in Norwood Cemetery yesterday afternoon, almost to the breaking of the hearts of his parents and other relatives. I had a dear old friend with whom I have often stayed at Mentone. On Monday last she seemed as well as ever, and on Wednesday she too was dead. Last Friday week, I had a letter from a friend at Plymouth saying that he was coming up to see me, and asking at what hour I could meet him? I said, "Five in the afternoon." It was our honored friend, Mr. Serpell. He did not come, but I received a note to say that he was not quite well. On Monday he addressed the Chamber of Commerce, and while he was speaking he fell back, apparently in a fainting fit, and so died. I have, therefore, lost some who have always been good helpers and kind friends to me, and I seem to feel more than ever I did that I am living in a dying world. It might have been any one of you, it might have been myself. Come, then, and let us all seek the Lord at once; let us each one seek Him now. "If *thou* seek him, he will be found of thee." God grant it, for Jesus Christ's sake! Amen.

6

The Sower

Behold, a sower went forth to sow (Matthew 13:3).

This was a very important event. I do not say that it was important if you took the individual case alone; but if you took the multitudes of cases in which it was also true, it was overwhelmingly important in the aggregate: "A sower went forth to sow." Yes, Christ thinks it worth while to mention that a single sower went forth to sow—that a Christian man went out to address a meeting on a village green, or to conduct a Bible class, or to speak anywhere for the Lord. But when you think of the hundreds of preachers of the Gospel who go out to sow every Lord's day, and the myriads of teachers who go to instruct the children in our Sunday schools, it is, surely, in the aggregate, the most important event under heaven. You may omit, O recording angel, the fact that a warrior went forth to fight; it is far more important that you should record that "a sower went forth to sow." You may even forget that a man of science went into his laboratory, and made a discovery, for no discovery can equal in importance the usual processes of husbandry. Do you hear the song of the harvest home? Do you see the loaded wagons follow one another in a long line to the farmer's barn? If so, remember that there would be no harvest home if the sower went not forth to sow. As the flail is falling upon the wheat, or the threshing machine is making the grain to leap from among the chaff, and the miller's wheels are grinding merrily, and the women are kneading the dough, and the bread is set upon the table, and parents and children are fed to the full, do not forget that all this could never happen unless "a sower went forth to sow." On this action hinges the very life of man. Bread, which is the staff of his life, would be broken, and taken from him, and his life could not continue did not a sower still go forth to sow. This seems to me to prove that the event recorded in our text is of prime importance, and deserves to be chronicled there.

This sermon was taken from *The Metropolitan Tabernacle Pulpit* and was preach on Thursday evening, September 6, 1888.

And, dear friends, the spiritual sowing stands in the same relation to the spiritual world that the natural sowing occupies in the natural world. It is a most important thing that we should continually go forth to preach the Gospel. It may seem, to some people, a small matter that I should occupy this pulpit, and I shall not lay any undue importance upon that fact; yet eternity may not exhaust all that shall result from the preaching of the Gospel here; there may be souls, plucked like brands from the burning, saved with an everlasting salvation, lamps lit by the Holy Spirit that shall shine like stars in the firmament of God forever and ever. Who knows, O teacher, when you labor even among the infants, what the result of your teaching may be? Good corn may grow in very small fields. God may bless your simple words to the babes that listen to them. How do you know, O my unlettered brother, when you stand up in the cottage meeting to talk to a few poor folk about Christ, what may follow from that effort of yours. Life or death, heaven or hell, may depend upon the sowing of the good seed of the Gospel. It is, it must be, the most important event that can ever happen, if the Lord goes forth with you when you go forth as the sower went forth to sow. Hark to the songs of the angels; see the overflowing brightness and excessive glory of your Heavenly Father's face. He rejoices because souls are born to Christ; but how could there be this joy, in the ordinary course, and speaking after the manner of men, without the preaching of the Word? For it still pleases God, by the foolishness of preaching, to save them that believe. I shall not, therefore, make any apology for again preaching upon an event which is so important, even though it is recorded in such simple words: "A sower went forth to sow."

I am going to try to answer three questions concerning this sower. First, *who was he*? Secondly *what did he do*? And thirdly, *what was he at?*

Who Was This Sower?

We do not know anything at all about him except that he was a sower. His individuality seems to be swallowed up in his office. We do not know who his father was, or his mother, or his sister, or his brother; all we know is that he was a sower, and I do like to see a man who is so much a minister that he is nothing else but a minister. It does not matter who he is, or what he has, or what else he can do, if he does this one thing. He has lost his identity in his service, though he has also gained it over again in another way. He has lost his selfhood, and has become, once for all, a sower, and nothing but a sower.

Observe, dear friends, that *there are many personal matters which are quite unimportant*. It is not mentioned here whether he was a refined sower, or a rustic sower; and it does not matter which he was. So is it with the workers for Christ, God blesses all sorts of men. William Huntington, the coalheaver, brought many souls to Christ. Some have doubted this; but, in my early Christian days, I knew some of the excellent of the earth who were the spiritual children of the coal-heaver. Chalmers stood at the very opposite pole—a master of cultured gracious speech, a learned, well-trained man; and what multitudes Chalmers brought to Christ! So, whether it was Huntington or Chalmers does not matter: "A sower went forth to sow." One preacher talks like Rowland Hill, in very plain Saxon with a touch of humor; another, like Robert Hall, uses a grand style of speech, full of brilliant rhetoric, and scarcely ever condescending to men of low degree, yet God blessed both of them. What mattered it whether the speech was of the colloquial or of the oratorical order so long as God blessed it? The man preached the Gospel; exactly how he preached it need not be declared. He was a sower, he went forth to sow, and there came a glorious harvest from his sowing.

Now, my dear brother, you have begun earnestly to speak for Christ, but you are troubled because you cannot speak like Mr. So-and-so. Do not try to speak like Mr. So-and-so. You say, "I heard a man preach the other night; and when he had done, I thought I could never preach again." Well, it was very naughty, on your part, to think that. You ought rather to have said, "I will try to preach all the hotter now that I have heard one who preaches so much hotter than I can." Just feel that you have to sow the good seed of the kingdom; and, if you have not so big a hand as some sowers have, and cannot sow quite so much at a time, go and sow with your smaller hand, only mind that you sow the same seed, for so God will accept what you do. You are grieved that you do not know so much as some do, and that you have not the same amount of learning that they have. You regret that you have not the poetical faculty of some, or the holy ingenuity of others. Why do you speak about all these things. Our Lord Jesus Christ does not do so; He simply says, "A sower went forth to sow." He does not tell us how he was dressed; He mentions nothing about whether he was a black man, or a white man, or what kind of man he was; He tells us nothing about him except that he was a sower. Will you, my dear friend, try to be nothing but a soulwinner? Never mind about "idiosyncrasies," or whatever people call them. Go ahead, and sow the good seed, and God bless you in doing so!

Next notice that, as the various personal matters relating to the man are too unimportant to be recorded, *his name and his fame are not written in this Book.* Do you want to have your name put to everything that you do? Mind that God does not let you have your desire, and then say to you, "There, you have done that for yourself, so you can reward yourself for it." As far as ever you can, keep your own name out of all the work you do for the Lord. I used to notice in Paris that there was not a bridge or a public building without the letter *N* somewhere on it. Now, go through all the city and find an *N* if you can. Napoleon hoped his fame would live in imperishable marble, but he had written his name in sand after all; and if any one of us shall in our ministry think it the all-important matter to make our own name prominent, we are on the wrong track altogether. When George Whitefield was asked to start a new sect, he said, "I do not condemn my brother Wesley for what he has done, but I cannot do the same; let my name perish, but let Christ's name endure forever and ever." Do not be anxious for your name to go down to posterity, but be more concerned to be only remembered by what you have done, as this man is only remembered by Christ's testimony that he was a sower.

What he did, in his sowing, is some of it recorded, but only that which refers to his special work. Where his seed fell, how it grew or did not grow, and what came of it or did not come of it—that is all there; but nothing else about his life or history is there at all. I pray you, do not be anxious for anything that shall embalm your reputation. Embalming is for the dead; so the living may be content to let their name and fame be blown away by the same wind that blows it to them. What does our reputation matter, after all! It is nothing but the opinion or the breath of men, and that is of little or no value to the child of God. Serve God faithfully, and then leave your name and fame in His keeping. There is a day coming when the righteous shall shine forth as the sun in the kingdom of their Father.

We have no record of the name and the fame of this man, yet *we do know something about him*. We know that he must have been, first of all, an eater, or he never would have been a sower. The Gospel is seed for the sower, and bread for the eater; and every man who goes out to sow for God must first have been an eater. There is not a man on the face of the earth who treads the furrows of the field, and sows the seed, but must first have been an eater of bread; and there is not a true servant of God beneath the cope of heaven, but has first fed on the Gospel before he has preached it. If there be any who pretend to sow, but who have never themselves eaten, God have mercy upon them! What a desecration of the pulpit it is for a man to attempt to preach what he does not himself know! What a desecration it is of even a Sunday school class for an unconverted young man, or young woman, to be a teacher of others! I do not think such a thing ought to be allowed. Wherever it has been permitted, I charge any who have been trying to teach what they do not themselves know, to cry to God to teach them that they may not go and pretend to speak in the name of the Lord, to the children, until, first of all, Christ has spoken peace and pardon to their own hearts, and He has been formed in them the hope of glory. May every worker here put to himself the question, "Have I fed upon and enjoyed that good Word which I am professing to teach to others?"

Next, having been an eater, he must also have been a receiver. A sower cannot sow if he has not any seed. It is a mere mockery to go up and down a field, and to pretend to scatter seed out of an empty hand. Is there not a

great deal of so-called Christian work that is just like that! Those who
engage in it have not anything to give; and, therefore, they can give nothing. You cannot pump out of a man or a woman what is not there; and you
cannot preach or teach, in God's way, what is not first in your own heart.
We must receive the Gospel seed from God before we can sow it. The
sower went to his master's granary, and received so many bushels of
wheat, and he then went out, and sowed it. I am afraid that some would-
be sowers fail in this matter of being receivers. They are in a great hurry
to take a class, or to preach here, or there, or somewhere else, but there is
nothing in it all. What can there be in your speech but sounding brass, and
a tinkling cymbal, unless you have received the living Word from the living God, and are sent forth by Him to proclaim it to men?

A true sower, also, is a disseminator of the Word of God. No man is a
sower unless he scatters the truth. If he does not preach truth, he is not a
sower in the true meaning of that term. A man may go whistling up and
down the furrows, and people may mistake him for a sower, but he is not
really one; and if there is not, in what we preach, the real, solid truth of
God's Word—however prettily we may put our sweet nothings, we have
not been serving the Lord. We must really scatter the living seed, or else
we are not worthy of the title of sower.

We seem to know a little about this sower now, and we further know
that *he was one of a noble line.* What our Lord really said was, "THE
SOWER went forth to sow"; and I think I see Him coming forth out of the
ivory palaces, from the lone glory of His own eternal nature, going down
to Bethlehem, becoming a baby, waiting a while until the seed was ready,
and then standing by the Jordan, and by the hillside, and at Capernaum, and
Nazareth, and everywhere scattering those great seeds that have made the
wilderness and the solitary place to be glad, and the desert to rejoice and
blossom as the rose. See how all Christendom has sprung from the sowing
of that Man; and our glorious Lord has long been reaping, and this day is
reaping still, the harvest of the seed-sowing on the hillsides of Galilee. "The
Sower went forth to sow." Are you not glad to be in that noble line? Do
you not feel it to be a high honor, even if you are the very least of the
sowers, to be one of those who have sowed the Gospel of God?

But who are the sowers who came next? Men "of whom the world was
not worthy"—men who suffered for their Lord and Master, His apostles,
and those who received their word, and who were faithful even to death,
a goodly army of all sorts of people, old and young, rich and poor, wise
and unlettered. And there has always continued a band of sowers going
forth to sow—men who could not help doing it, like the tinker of Bedford,
to wit. They commanded him not to sow any more of the seed, and they
cast him into prison because he would still do it but, through the window
of that prison he kept on sowing great handfuls of seed which are, even

now, falling upon the broad acres of our own and other lands. When they bade him be quiet, he said, "If you let me out of prison today, I will preach again tomorrow, by the grace of God." "Oh, then!" they answered, "go back to your cell, sir." "Yes," he said, "and I will lie there until the moss grows on my eyelids, before I will make you any promise that I will be silent." He must sow, he could not help it. Well, now, today, it is imagined by some that the new theology is to put an end to our sowing of the good seed of the kingdom; but will it? I believe that the sowers will still go to every lane and alley of the city, and to every hamlet and village of our country, when God wills it, for the Gospel is as everlasting as the God who gave it, and, therefore, it cannot die out; and when they think that they have killed the plant, it will spring up everywhere more vigorous than before.

The sower is not only a man of an honorable line, but he is also a worker together with God. It is God's design that every plant should propagate and reproduce its like; especially is it His design that wheat, and other cereals so useful to men, should be continued and multiplied on the face of the earth. Who is to do it? God will see that it is done; usually, He employs men to be His agents. There are some seeds that never can be sown by men, but only by birds. I need not go into the details, but it is a fact that no man could make the seed grow if he did sow it; it must be done by a bird. But as to wheat, man must sow that; you cannot go into any part of the world and find a field of wheat unless a man has sown the seed to produce it. You may find fields full of thistles, but wheat must be sown. It is not a wild thing, it must have a man to care for it. God, therefore, links Himself with man in the continuance of wheat on the face of the earth; He has so arranged that, while He could spread the Gospel by His Spirit without human voices, while He could bring untold myriads to Himself without any instrumentality, yet He does not do so, and as means to the end He has in view, He intends YOU to speak, that He may speak through you, and that, in the speaking, the seed may be scattered, which He shall make to bring forth an abundant harvest.

What Did This Sower Do?

Now, secondly, what did this sower do? He "went forth." I am going to dwell upon that fact for a few minutes.

I think this means, first, that *he bestirred himself*. He said, "It is time that I went forth to sow. I have waited quite long enough for favorable weather, but I remember that Solomon said, 'He that observeth the wind shall not sow.' I feel that the sowing time has come for me, and I must set about it." Can I look upon some here, who have been members of the church for years, but who have never yet done anything for the Lord? Brother or sister, if you have been a servant of God for many years, and have never yet really worked for the salvation of souls, I want you now just to say to yourself, "Come now, I must get at this work," You will be going home soon; when your Master says to you, "Did you do any sowing for Me?" you will have to reply, "No, Lord; I did plenty of eating. I went to the Tabernacle, and I enjoyed the services." "But did you do any sowing?" "No, Lord; I did a great deal of hoarding; I laid up a large quantity of the good seed." "But did you do any sowing?" He will still ask, and that will be a terrible question for those who never went forth to sow. You are very comfortable at home, are you not? In the long winter evenings that are coming on, it will be so pleasant to enjoy yourselves at home of an evening. There, stir the fire, and draw the curtain close, and let us sit down, and spend a happy time. Yes, but is it not time for you, Mr. Sower, to go forth? The millions of London are perishing; asylums for the insane are filling, jails are filling, poverty is abounding, and drunkenness is at every street corner. Harlotry is making good men and women to blush. It is time to set about work for the Lord if I am ever to do it. What are some of you doing for God? Oh, that you would begin to take stock of your capacity, or your incapacity, and say, "I must get to work for the Master. I am not to spend my whole life thinking about what I am going to do; I must do the next thing, and do it at once, or I may be called home, and my day be over before I have sown a single handful of wheat."

Next, *the sower quitted his privacy*. He came out from his solitude, and began to sow. This is what I mean. At first, a Christian man very wisely lives indoors. There is a lot of cleaning and scrubbing to be done there. When the bees come out of their cells, they always spend the first few days of their lives in the hive cleaning and getting everything tidy. They do not go out to gather honey until they have first of all done the housework at home. I wish that all Christian people would get their housework done as soon as they can. It needs to be done. I mean, acquaintance with experimental matters of indwelling sin, and overcoming grace. But, after that, the sower went forth to sow. He was not content with his own private experience, but he went forth to sow. There are numbers of people who are miserable because they are always at home. They have cleaned up everything there, even to the bottoms of the saucepans outside, and now they do not know what to do; so they begin blacking them over again, and cleaning them once more; always at work upon the little trifles of their own kitchen. Go out, brother; go out, sister. Important as your experience is, it is only important as a platform for real usefulness. Get all right within, in order that you may get to work without.

The sower, when he went forth to sow, also *quitted his occupation of a learner and an enjoyer of the truth*. He was in the Bible class for a year or two, and he gained a deal of Scriptural knowledge there. He was also a regular hearer of the Word. You could see him regularly sitting in his pew, and drinking in the Word; but, after a while, he said to himself, "I have no right to remain in this Bible class; I ought to be in the Sunday school, and take a class myself." Then he said to himself, on a Sunday evening, "I have been to one service today, and have been spiritually fed, so I think I ought to go to one of the lodging houses in the Mint, and speak to the people there, or find some other holy occupation in which I can be doing some good to others." So he went forth to sow, and I want to stir you all up to do this. Perhaps I do not need to say much upon this matter to my own people here, but there are also many strangers with us. I would like to do with you what Samson did with the foxes and firebrands. We have far too many professing Christians who are doing next to nothing. If I could send you among the standing corn of some of the churches, to set them on fire, it would not be a bad Thursday evening's work.

"A sower went forth to sow." Where did he come from? I do not know what house he came from, but I tell you the place from which he last came. *He came out of the granary.* He must have been to the granary to get the seed. At least, if he did not go there before he went to sow, he did not have anything that was worth sowing. O my dear brothers and sisters, especially my brethren in the ministry, we must always go to the granary, must we not? Without the diligent and constant study of Scripture, of what use will our preaching be? "I went into the pulpit," said one, "and I preached straight off just what came into my mind, and thought nothing of it." "Yes," said another, "and your people thought nothing of it, too." That is sure to be the case. You teachers, who go to your classes quite unprepared, and open your Bible, and say just what comes first, should remember that God does not want your nonsense. "Oh, but!" says one, "it is not by human wisdom that souls are saved." No, nor is it by human ignorance. But if you profess to teach, do learn. He can never be a teacher who is not first a learner. I am sure that, when the sower went forth to sow, the last place he came from was the granary; and mind that you go to the granary, too, dear worker.

I wonder whether this sower did what I recommend every Christian sower to do, namely, to come forth from *the place where he had steeped his seed.* One farmer complained that his wheat did not grow, and another asked him, "Do you steep your seed?" "No," he replied, "I never heard of such a thing." The first one said, "I steep mine in prayer, and God prospers me." If we always steep our heavenly seed in prayer, God will prosper us also. For a solitary man to stand up and preach is poor work; but for two of us to be here, is grand work. You have heard the story of the Welsh preacher who had not arrived when the service ought to have been begun, and his host sent a boy to the room to tell him that it was time to go to preach. The boy came hurrying back, and said, "Sir, he is in his room, but I do not think he is coming. There is somebody in there with him. I heard him speaking very loudly, and very earnestly, and I heard him say that if that other person did not come with him, he would not come at all, and the other one never answered him, so I do not think he will come." "Ah!" said the host, who understood the case, "He will come, and the other one will come with him." Oh! it is good sowing when the sower goes forth to sow, and the other comes with him! Then we go forth with steeped seed, seed that is sprouting in our hands as we go forth. This does not happen naturally, but it does happen spiritually. It seems to grow while we are handling it, for there is life in it; and when it is sown, there will be life in it to our hearers.

Further, this sower *went forth into the open field.* Wherever there was a field ready for the sowing, there he came. Beloved friends, we must always try to do good where there is the greatest likelihood of doing good. I do not think that I need to go anywhere else than here, for here are the people to whom I can preach; but if this place was not filled with people, I would feel that I had no right to stand here, and preach to empty pews. If it is so in your little chapel, if the people do not come—I do not desire that the chapel should be burnt down, but it might be a very mitigated calamity if you had to turn out into the street to preach, or if you had to go to some hall or barn, for some people might come and hear you there who will never hear you now. You must go forth to sow. You cannot sit at your parlor window, and sow wheat; and you cannot stand on one little plot of ground, and keep on sowing there. If you have done your work in that place, go forth to sow elsewhere. Oh, that the church of Christ would go forth into heathen lands! Oh, that there might be, among Christians, a general feeling that they must go forth to sow! What a vast acreage there still is upon which not a grain of God's wheat has ever yet fallen! Oh, for a great increase of the missionary spirit! May God send it upon the entire church until everywhere it shall be said, "Behold, a sower went forth to sow." There is a "behold" in my text, which I have saved up until now: "Behold, a sower went forth to sow." He went as far as ever he could to sow the good seed, that his master might have a great harvest from it; let us go and do likewise.

When did this man go forth to sow? Our farming friends begin to sow very soon after harvest That is the time to sow for Christ. As soon as ever you have won one soul for Him, try and win another by God's grace. Say to yourself what the general said to his troops when some of them came riding up, and said, "Sir, we have captured a gun from the enemy." "Then," said he, "go and capture another." After the reaping, let the sowing follow as speedily as possible. In season, this sower sowed. It is a great thing to observe the proper season for sowing, but it is a greater thing to sow in improper seasons also, for out of season is sometimes the best season for God's sower to sow. "Be instant in season, out of season," was Paul's exhortation to Timothy. Oh, for grace to be always sowing! I have known good men to go about, and never to be without tracts to give away, and suitable tracts, too. They seem to have picked them out, and God has given them an occasion suitable for the tracts; or if they have not given tracts, they have been ready with a good word, a choice word, a loving word, a tender word. There is a way of getting the Gospel in edgewise, when you cannot get it in at the front. Wise sowers sow their seed broadcast, yet I have generally noticed that they never sow against the wind, for that would blow the dust into their eyes; and there is nothing like sowing with the wind. Whichever way the Holy Spirit seems to be moving, and Providence is also moving, scatter your seed that the wind may carry it as far as possible, and that it may fall where God shall make it grow.

Thus I have told you what the man did: "A sower went forth to sow."

What Was This Sower At?

On this occasion, he did not go forth *to keep the seed to himself.* He went forth to throw it to the wind; he threw it away from himself, scattered it far and wide. He did not go out to defend it; he threw it about, and left it to take its chance. He did not go, at this time, to examine it, to see whether it was good wheat, or not. No doubt he had done that before; but he just scattered it. He did not go out to winnow it, and blow away the chaff, or pick out any darnel that might be in it. That was all done at home. Now he has nothing to do but to sow it, *to sow it*, TO SOW IT; and he sows it with all his might. He did not even come to push others out of the field who might be sowing bad seed, but he took occasion, at this particular time, to go forth to sow, and to do nothing else.

> One thing at a time, and that done well,
> Is a very good rule, as many can tell;

and it is especially so in the service of God. Do not try to do twenty things at once: "A sower went forth to sow." *His object was a limited one.* He did not go forth to make the seed grow. No, that was beyond his power; he went forth to sow. If we were responsible for the effect of the Gospel upon the hearts of men, we would be in a sorry plight indeed: but we are only responsible for the sowing of the good seed. If you hear the Gospel, dear friends, and reject it, that is your act, and not ours. If you are saved by it, give God the glory; but if it proves to be a savor of death unto death to you, yours is the sin, the shame, and the sorrow. The preacher cannot save souls, so he will not take the responsibility that does not belong to him.

And the sower did not, at that time, go forth to reap. There are many instances in which the reaper has overtaken the sower, and God has saved souls on the spot while we have been preaching. Still, what this man went forth to do was to sow. Whether there is any soul saved or not, our business is to preach the Gospel, the whole Gospel, and nothing but the Gospel; we must keep to this one point, preaching Jesus Christ, and Him crucified. That is sowing the seed. We cannot create the harvest; that will come in God's own time.

This man's one object was positively before him, and we are to impart the truth, to make known to men the whole of the Gospel. You are lost, God is gracious, Christ has come to seek and to save that which is lost. Whosoever believes in Him shall not perish, but shall have everlasting life. On the cross He offered the sacrifice by which sin is put away. Believe in Him, and you live by His death. This sowing, you see, is simply telling out the truth; and this is the main thing that we have to do, dear friends, to keep on telling the same truth over, and over, and over, and over again, until we get it into the minds and hearts of men, and they receive it through God's blessing. If the sower had sat down at the corner of the field, and played the harp all day, he would not have done his duty; and if, instead of preaching the simple Gospel, we talk of the high or deep mysteries of God, we shall not have done our duty. The sower's one business is to sow; so, stick to your sowing, brothers and sisters. When that is done, and your Master calls you home, He will find you other work to do for Him in heaven; but, for the present, this is to be your occupation.

Now, to close, let me remind you that *sowing is an act of faith.* If a man had not great faith in God, he would not take the little wheat he has, and go and bury it. His good wife might say to him, "John, we shall want that corn for the children, so don't you go and throw it out where the birds may eat it, or the worms destroy it." And you must preach the Gospel, and you must teach the Gospel, as an act of faith. You must believe that God will bless it. If not, you are not likely to get a blessing upon it. If it is done merely as a natural act, or a hopeful act, that will not be enough; it must be done as an act of confidence in the living God. He bids you speak the Word, and makes you His lips for the time, and He says that His Word shall not return to Him void, but that it shall prosper in the thing whereto He has sent it.

This sowing was also *an act of energy.* The word *sower* is meant to describe an energetic man. He was, as we say, "all there." So, when we teach Christ, we must teach Him with all our might, throwing our very souls into our teaching. O brothers, never let the Gospel hang on our lips like icicles! Let it rather be like burning lava from the mouth of a volcano; let us be all on fire with the divine truth that is within our hearts, sowing it with all the heart, and mind, and soul, and strength.

This sowing was also *an act of concentrated energy.* The sower "went forth TO SOW." He went forth, not with two aims or objects, but with this one; not dividing his life into a multitude of channels, but making all run in one strong, deep current, along this one riverbed.

Now I have done when I invite my brothers and sisters here to go forth from this Tabernacle to sow. You will go down those front steps, or you will go out at the back doors, and scatter all over London. I know not how far you may be going, but let it be written of you tonight, "The sowers went forth to sow"—they went forth from the Tabernacle with one resolve that, by the power of the living Spirit of God, they who are redeemed with the precious blood of Jesus would make known His Gospel to the sons of men, sowing that good seed in every place wherever they have the opportunity, trusting in God to make the seed increase and multiply. Ah, but do not forget to do it even within these walls, for there are some here whom you may never be able to get at again. So, if you can speak to your neighbor in the pew, say a good word for Christ. If you will begin to be sowers, nothing is better than to begin at once. Throw a handful before you get outside the door; who knows whether that first handful shall not be more successful than all you have sown, or shall sow, in after days?

As for you, dear souls, who have never received the living seed, oh, that you would receive it at once! May God, the Holy Spirit, make you to be like well-prepared ground that opens a thousand mouths to take in the seed and then encloses the seed within itself, and makes it fructify! May God bless you; may He never leave you barren or unfruitful, but may you grow a great harvest to His glory, for Christ's sake! Amen.

7

Bringing Sinners to the Savior

And one of the multitude answered and said, Master, I have brought unto thee my son, which hath a dumb spirit; and wheresoever he taketh him, he teareth him: and he foameth, and gnasheth with his teeth, and pineth away: and I spake to thy disciples that they should cast him out; and they could not. He answereth him, and saith, O faithless generation, how long shall I be with you? how long shall I suffer you? bring him unto me. And they brought him unto him: and when he saw him, straightway the spirit tare him; and he fell on the ground, and wallowed foaming (Mark 9:17–20).

I do not intend to speak so much upon the whole of this text as to use the latter part of it as a sort of motto for an appeal to Christian people to be diligent in the service of their Lord. If we wish to do good to our fellow-creatures, the best thing that we can do for them is to bring them to the Lord Jesus Christ. At the feet of Jesus we ourselves obtained salvation if we are saved. We never had any true peace of heart until we came to Christ, and we never would have had any if we had remained apart from Him. The great Physician, who healed our soul-sickness, was Christ Jesus the Lord; and if we are to be the means of blessing to the sons of men, we must recommend to them the Physician whom we have proved to be so exceedingly useful to ourselves. They cannot be blessed, any more than we could be, until they are brought to Jesus.

When any of us desire to be of service to others, it is well for us to learn the best way of setting about our task; for if we do not know how to go to work, all our earnestness may be expended upon that which is useless; but when we understand what we are at, and concentrate all our powers upon

This sermon was taken from *The Metropolitan Tabernacle Pulpit* and was preached on Sunday evening, August 22, 1880.

wise and proper efforts, then are we likely to succeed. To my mind, the first thing that we have to strive after, in the name of God, and by the help of the Holy Spirit, is to bring men to Jesus Christ.; and God forbid that we should ever lift even a finger to point them anywhere else for salvation. Each true believer, as well as every Christian minister, should say—

> 'Tis all my business here below
> To cry, "Behold the Lamb!"

We are to point sinners to Jesus—ourselves looking at Him all the while, and praying that they also may look to Him, and live.

I think I need hardly remind you that every Christian is bound to give himself to the blessed work of bringing sinners to the Savior. Common humanity should lead us to attempt this task. Is it necessary for me to bid you love your fellows, and seek their good? Why, even they who have no Christianity are often exceedingly generous, and humane, and kind. Some persons whose religious opinions are full of error, have, nevertheless, manifested great tenderness and sympathy toward the sick, and the suffering, and the poor; they have set a noble example of what others might do for the needy. Much more, then, ought the followers of the loving Christ to have tender, sympathetic hearts, and anxiously to desire to do the most they can for their fellow men. I shall take it for granted, my dear hearers, that you, who are members of this church, or of any other true Christian church, are desirous to be the means of blessing to those who are about you, and that you also believe that the surest way to bless them is to bring them to Christ.

Parents Are the First Persons Who Should Labor to Bring Their Children to Christ

In the 17th verse, we read that *the epileptic youth was, in a sense, brought to Christ by his father.* "Master," said the poor man, "I have brought unto thee my son, which hath a dumb spirit." He hardly knew how to set to work, for he somehow confounded Christ with His disciples; so, as the Lord Jesus was away upon the mountain, he brought his son to the disciples. They could not cast out the devil, yet it was a right thing, on the part of the father, to bring his child to them; it showed a loving spirit, and a desire to see him cured. I am afraid there are some fathers, who even call themselves Christians, who have not yet done as much for their sons and daughters as that father did for his boy, for they have not asked for the sympathy and help of Christian people on behalf of their own children. I am utterly ashamed of some professors of religion who say that they really must leave that matter to their children. I have heard of one man who said that he did not like to prejudice his boy, so he would not say anything to him about religion. The devil, however, was quite willing to prejudice the lad, so very early in life he learned to swear, although his father had a foolish and wicked objection to teaching him to pray. If you ever feel it incumbent upon you not to prejudice a piece of ground by sowing good seed in it, you may rest assured that the weeds will not imitate your impartiality, but they will take possession of the land in a very sad and shocking manner. Where the plow does not go, and the seed is not sown, the weeds are quite sure to multiply, and if children are left untutored and untrained, all sorts of evils will spring up in their hearts and lives.

If a professedly Christian parent has not even put his children under godly tuition, what shall I say of him? He must be a Christian watered down to a very low point, or beaten out to extreme thinness. There must be very little, if any, grace left in such a man as that. We have known wealthy Christian men send their boys to school where the whole influence was altogether against religion, or else utterly neutral. Girls have sometimes been sent abroad to learn a foreign language in the midst of those who are steeped in gross error, and it does not seem to have occurred to the parents that they ought first to have cared about the souls of their daughters. Oh, dear me! are such people as these worthy to be called Christians at all; or do they merely wear the Christian label upon their breasts without having the grace of God in their hearts? Dear brother or sister, if you cannot speak to your own children altogether as you can wish about their souls, do follow the example of this man, and bring your dear ones to the disciples that they may see what they can do for them in the Master's name. Still, recollect that there was a mistake in this father's action, because, at first, he made the disciples the terminus of his journey instead of merely coming to them *en route* to Christ. We may make Christian men the way by which we try to get to Christ; but to stop at them, and not to bring the children to Christ Himself, will be fatal to all our desire for the salvation of their souls.

This man did not see his child cured by the disciples, *yet he persevered after his first failure*. "Master," said he, "I have brought unto thee my son, which hath a dumb spirit. . . . I spake to thy disciples that they should cast him out; and they could not." In effect, he said, "They have failed, so I have brought him to You." So, if the Sunday school teacher has not been blessed to your girl—if the instruction in that Bible class, to which she has gone for years, has not been the means of her conversion—if your boy after having had the best religious training, remains unsaved, go straight away to the great Master in your earnest prayers, and so bring your dear children to Christ. I am not a believer in the theory that some hold—that children do not grow up in the fear of God if they have been trained in it. It is true that there have been many ministers sons who have been ungodly young men, I have had very sad proof of that fact; yet I fear that some of those ministers may have neglected their own families while they were preaching to others. It is very easy for a man—especially if his wife does not help him to train their children aright—to neglect the affairs of his own family while he is continually busy about the work of the church; thus they are not trained up in the way they should go. I wish that this evil was not so common as it is; but I do know that some have grown up ungodly because there was not due attention paid to them. The vineyard at home was neglected while other people's vineyards were being kept.

If you have no family prayer, and your children do not grow up to be Christians, how can you expect that they will? If there is no altar in the house, is it right to call it God's house at all? Wherever Abraham pitched his tent, he built an altar too; and that is the custom of all those who live near to God, they sanctify their dwellings with daily prayer and praise; but if that practice is neglected, and the father keeps his religion in the background, and does not let it be seen at home, I do not marvel if his boys and girls grow up to say that there is nothing in it. It is a sad thing when children can say, "Father made a profession of religion, but his life was not consistent with it. Mother also professed to be a Christian, but we never heard her speak of Christ. She never prayed with us, or, in our hearing, for us." Where no influence is used, it is not probable that there can be any result. I told you the other night of a dear brother who said, when I exhorted my hearers to select somebody to pray for, that he had prayed for one person for twenty years, and that he is not converted yet. So I said to him, "Have you spoken to your friend personally about his soul? Have you made it your business to go down to his house, and tell him that you are anxious about him?" "No," he replied, "I cannot say that I have done so." "Well, then," I asked, "do you expect God to hear prayers of that kind? Suppose I were to pray that it might be a good harvest over in that field, and yet, for twenty years, I did not sow any corn there; the probability is that, when I did sow some, I should get my prayers answered, and gather in the harvest." If we pray for anything, God expects us to use the proper means of obtaining it; and if we neglect the means, we have no right to expect Him to believe in the sincerity of our prayer. If a father and mother pray for their children, but never pray with them, or speak to them personally about the welfare of their souls, they must not wonder if they are not brought to Christ.

Each One of Us May Help in the Blessed
Work of Bringing Children to Christ

But, secondly, although parents should be the first persons to bring their children to Christ, we may, each one of us, help in this blessed work. Our text says, "*They* brought him unto him"; that is, the disciples helped the father to bring this poor epileptic child to Jesus.

In seeking to bring sinners to the Savior, we shall find that *some are brought to Him by almost unconscious influence.* I believe that when a man is full of the grace of God, he is like a Leyden jar that is charged with electricity; if he possesses true holiness, he will give some of it to others almost without knowing that he is doing so. I have met with many singular instances of that indirect way of doing good. Some three or four months ago, there was a working man, whose wife, being suddenly taken ill, needed a certain Christian woman to come and attend her. The husband went to her house to try to find her. It was on a Sunday evening, so she was where she ought to be at that time, in the house of God, in a little chapel not many miles from here. The man knew that he must have this good woman to go to his wife, so he went to the chapel, and as he could not get her at once, he waited for a few minutes, and listened to the preacher. He was interested in what he heard, so he went to that chapel again the next Sunday morning. Before long he was brought to know the Lord, and now he has joined the church, and by his earnest work is a great help to the minister. Well, now, if that good woman had not been a Christian, she might not have been in that chapel. If she had not been a regular attendant on the means of grace, she would not have been there, and the man would not have had to go to the place where he found blessing to his soul.

I know of another case that may seem equally strange. A man and his wife went to live in a certain street where nobody, to their knowledge, attended any place of worship. It is dreadful to think that in London you may go into street after street where a person, who goes to either a church or a meeting house, is quite an exception to the general rule; it is sad that it should be so, but so it certainly is. These two people regularly went to a place of worship, and it happened there was living in the same street a man who, when he resided in the country, was a regular attendant on the means of grace; and, as these people went by his window, Sunday after Sunday, although they did not know him, and never said a word to him, and were even quite unconscious of their influence over him, they were preaching to him by their action, for it rebuked him, and he said to himself, "What would my mother think if she knew how I spend my Sundays? There are two good people, who are just like my father and mother at home, who, about this time, are going to the meeting house." He brushed himself up for the evening service, found his way to the house of God, and soon became a Christian.

When you are doing anything that is right, you cannot tell how much blessing you are scattering. Any man or woman, a master or a servant, may be of essential service in bringing others to Jesus, simply by a happy, cheerful, kind, gentle behavior. You may not have the opportunity of saying much for Christ; perhaps it might not be proper in your position that you should do so; but those about you watch you, they note your genial spirit, and they begin to like you. They observe your consideration for others, and they admire it; then they see your cheerfulness, and they wonder what is the secret of it. Possibly, you are ill, and someone comes to visit you; you are very patient, you even sing in the midst of your pain. Persons who see and hear you, and who note how you bear it all, say to themselves, "There is something within these people that we do not understand"; and thus you exercise an influence over them although you may have said very little to them. The fact that you are a Christian is one of the most practical and powerful means of bringing others to inquire what this religion is which elevates, sweetens, softens, and yet strengthens, and makes people to be manifestly like their Father in heaven.

I remember hearing Mr. Jay, of Bath, tell the story of a good girl, a servant, who attended his meeting house. Her master and mistress were very strict church people, and when they found out that Jane went to the meeting house, they talked to her very roughly, and said that she must give up going there. She answered very gently that she must go where her own soul was fed, and she could not meet their wishes in that matter, though she was willing to do so in everything else. "Very well, Jane," they replied, "then you must take a month's notice, for we cannot have any of these horrible Dissenters living with us." That evening, as the lady and gentleman sat talking together, one of them said, "She is really a good girl, do you not think we are treating her very badly? Suppose she were to insist that we should go to the meeting house with her, we would say that it was very wrong for her to tyrannize over us, so is it not wrong for us to try to tyrannize over her?" "She took it so gently, too," said the other. "We would not have stood it as she did. Suppose we go and see what this Mr. Jay is like whom she goes to hear; for if he is a good man, she may as well go to the meeting house as to the church." They went; and, in telling the story, Mr. Jay said, "They have continued to come and hear Mr. Jay up to the present time." So, you see that the servant had, by her consistent Christian character, brought her master and mistress round to her way of thinking, although they could not coerce her to theirs; and you can judge what influence you also may exert over others if you have the grace of God abounding in you. May God fill us full of it that we may be the means of bringing many sinners to the Savior! Yet we must not be content with unconscious influence, and I hope none of us will be like the young gentleman who advertised that he would like board and lodging where his Christian example would be considered to be an equivalent for what he received.

In many instances, much good has been done in bringing souls to Christ *by casual seed-sowing*. Eternity alone will disclose the good results that have sometimes followed from the utterance of one short word. I trace all the light I have upon a certain subject to a remark made by the usher in a school where I was many years ago; he was teaching geography, and he let drop a sentence, which I need not repeat, but I remember it to this day, and it had an influence upon my whole after career and character. I also recollect a few gracious words that were spoken to me by a godly old woman, who used to read her

Gospel Herald, and talk to me about the power of divine grace. I rejoiced to get a grip of the grand old Calvinistic doctrine, very much through half a dozen sentences that fell from the lips of that poor, humble, Christian woman, whom it was my great happiness to help, in later years, when she was in poverty. I felt that I owed so much to her that I must do anything I could to comfort her. You will often prove that, as George Herbert says—

A verse may find him who a sermon flies—

and that a short sentence may strike and stick where a long address may altogether fall flat. Give away a tract whenever you can; better still, give a little book that will not be torn up, one that has a cover on it, for you will probably see it upon the table when you call again. Speak a word for the Master whenever it is possible, and offer a short prayer at every convenient opportunity. I think we should make it a rule, whenever we hear a foul or blasphemous word in the street (and, alas! we constantly do so), always to pray for the person who utters it. Perhaps then the devil might find it expedient not to stir up people to swear, if he knew that it excited Christians to pray. Try it, at all events, and see whether it may not have a subtle power to stop the profanity which is so terribly on the increase.

Over and above all this indirect service, there ought to be *direct effort, made by all Christians, for the conversion of those around them.* Try what you can each one do by personally addressing other people. I have heard of one, an utter stranger to religion, who was brought to Christ through a gentleman tapping him on the shoulder, and saying to him, "Well, my brother, how does your soul prosper today?" The one to whom he spoke turned around, having never heard such a question before, and the other, as he saw his face, exclaimed, "I beg a thousand pardons; I thought you were my old friend So-and-so, who has been in the habit of putting that question to me." It was a mistake, but it was a very blessed mistake, for the Spirit of God used it to the awakening of a conscience that was lying dormant, an honest conscience, which only needed to be aroused by some such startling inquiry as that. Dear friends, do try to speak personally to some friends about their immortal souls. I know that it is not easy work for some of you to break the ice and make a beginning in such service, but I can assure you that you will do it better and better the more often you attempt it.

Beside that, bring people to the means of grace definitely with a view to their conversion. Help me all you can in trying to preach to the people. Get any, in whom you are concerned, to come to the house of God. A young man, who grew up to be a most useful minister of Christ, had been entirely careless about divine things until a neighbor said to him, "I have a sitting in the Tabernacle; if you will come with me, you can use my ticket." The friend who made that kind suggestion stood all the service through where he could see the young man, and he was earnestly praying for him all the while. The result of lending his seat, on that one occasion, was that the young man was brought to the Savior; he was soon in the Sunday school as a teacher, and, afterward, as I told you, he became a most useful minister. Are there not more of you who might try that plan? I know that some of you have done this; then do it over and over again. Deny yourself of a Christian privilege for the sake of bringing others where the Lord will be likely to meet with them, especially if you back up the preacher's word with your continual prayer on behalf of those whom you have brought to listen to his message.

Then, if you really want to bring souls to Christ, remember that there are the young to be taught. Just now, all our schools are languishing for lack of teachers. O you, who would have your crown studded with gems, seek them among the little ones! It is a happy task, however arduous it may be, so give yourselves to it with your whole hearts and souls. Others of you, if you do not feel called to take a class of children, might sometimes speak words of warning to the grosser sinners with whom you come into contact, and words of encouragement to those who are seeking the Savior. There is many and many a poor sinner, floundering in the Slough of Despond, who only wants someone, rightly named Help, to come and point out to him where the stepping-stones are, or to lend him a hand lest he should altogether sink under his crushing burden of guilt.

This I know, dear Christian friends: if you are not trying to bring sinners to the Savior, you are missing the chief end of your being, and you are also missing the most joyous work that can ever occupy your attention. Oh, if you bring a soul to Jesus, the joy of it is unspeakable! I have before my mind's eye at this moment, a little cottage in the country, in which lived the first person of whom I heard that I had been the means of bringing her to Jesus. After preaching for some little time, I wanted some seal to my service; and when the deacon of the little church of which I was the minister said to me, "There was a poor woman cut to the quick the other Sunday night; and I believe she has found the Savior," I posted off directly to see her. Those of you who have had a similar experience can imagine the joy I had in hearing her tell the story. She went home years ago, perhaps the first of those who have gone to heaven, whom God has called by my means; but I was so glad, so happy, so delighted with my first convert that I say to you, "Do seek the same joy, if you yourself know the Lord."

So that is my second point, that all of us, who are believers in Christ, may bring others to him.

There Are Some Occasions That Need United Exertions

God, the Holy Spirit, of course does the whole work in the conversion of a soul, but He works by instrumentalities, and there are some desperate cases in which He does not work upon a soul through one instrument alone, but He moves a number of persons to act together to that end. Our text says, "*They* brought him unto him." This poor youth was foaming and gnashing with his teeth, and tearing himself just as you have seen persons do in an epileptic fit, so that it took several persons to hold him; together they grasped him, and, with one desperate, united effort, they brought him to the feet of Jesus, and Jesus cast out the evil spirit and healed the poor sufferer.

In this way, *people and minister may unite in bringing sinners to the Savior.* There may be some persons who come here who will never be converted until you and I join in seeking their salvation. Somebody must preach, but other bodies must pray; and if a score of you should be praying about any one person in the congregation, I believe that it will not be long before that epileptic is cured. The devil himself shall be defeated by the united prayers of many believers, especially if they are those mighty prayers of which our Savior spoke when He said, "This kind goeth not out but by prayer and fasting"—when the praying souls hunger for the salvation of the suffering one, and unitedly cry to God to effect it. We have had much happy union in Christian work, let us have more of it; say to one another, "While the pastor preaches, we will pray; nay, more than that, we will continually remember him in our prayers, for we know that he needs them, and prizes them." That is quite true, dear friends; for it is no small thing to minister every Sunday to this great company of people, and then, through the printed page, to address tens of thousands of readers, even to the utmost ends of the earth. Yes, I do indeed need your prayers and your help; give them to me, for then we may be sure that "they"—that is, all of us together, shall bring many to Jesus.

Another form of cooperation is when there is a soul that has been prayed for, but no answer has come, so you call a few praying people to meet in your house, and you tell them the details of the case, and make a point of praying specially for that person. I have known instances in which brethren have collected a score of Christian friends, who, perhaps, never before met in one place; but they pledged themselves to pray about one particular case; and their united prayers have, with God's blessing, accomplished what previously seemed to be impossible. It has been truly said that if you have a very hard thing, you can cut it with something harder; and if any heart is especially hard, God can use the hard, strong, persistent vehemence of other mighty, passionate souls to pray the blessing of eternal life into that stubborn, rebellious heart. I would like to hear more frequently of friends banding themselves together, and meeting in their private houses to pray about somebody or other, making the person about whom they are interested the subject of special supplication; that would be the way to bring him to Jesus.

Then, *add to that prayer, distinct united effort.* Perhaps, if one friend would speak to that person, he may resent it. Then, if another would address him, he may receive it coolly. But when another speaks to him, he may begin to listen a little more attentively; and the next one may be able to put the key into the keyhole and be the means, in the hand of God, of opening the closed door of that man's heart. If God moves us to join in effort for any soul, I do not believe that we shall often find it to be a failure. At any rate, if a man will go down to hell, I would like that we should make it very difficult for him to get there; if he will not turn to Christ, I would that we were resolved that it should not be for want of being prayed for, or for lack of being earnestly pleaded with. We will be clear of his blood; we will shake off the very dust of our feet against such as determine to remain impenitent, and resolve that, to the utmost of our capacity, Christ shall be set forth, so that, if men reject Him at all, they shall willfully reject Him.

Oh, that my words' might stir up all of you who profess to be Christians. We have over five thousand church members—nearly six thousand. Oh, if all were alive to God and earnest in His service—"all at it, and always at it"—what might not be done, God the Holy Spirit blessing our labors? But, alas! there are many people here, like the camp followers of an army, who do not fight when the battle comes on. Those who do the fighting are often hampered by these other people, and, sometimes, they almost feel as if they wanted to clear the ground of such loiterers and hinderers; instead of doing that, I beg all of you, dear friends, to wake up, and see what you can do for the Christ who has done so much for you. Let us all ask to be aroused again, and to be thoroughly stirred up in the service of the Savior. God grant that this south of London—and the north, and west, and east, too—may be permeated and saturated with your earnest endeavors to bring sinners to the Savior! The Lord bless you, for Christ's sake! Amen.

8

Scales Taken from the Eyes

And immediately there fell from his eyes as it had been scales (Acts 11:18).

This means that the film upon Saul's eyes was comparable to the scales of a fish, or else that it fell off as scales might fall. When the blinding film was gone, light broke into the darkness of Saul. In different men, sin manifests its chief power in different parts of their natures. In the case of many, sin is most apparent in their eyes; that is to say, ignorance, error, and prejudice have injured their mental sight. Some have the withered hand of conscious inability, others have the deaf ear of mental obtuseness; but there are far more who hear the joyful sound, and display much energy, but they hear without understanding, and are zealous without knowledge, for they are blind. This was Saul's condition. He was thoroughly honest: we might say of his heart, when it was at its worst, that it was always true to its convictions. He was no deceiver, and no timeserver. He went in for what he believed to be right with all his might; lukewarmness and selfish policy were alien to his nature. He dashed with all his might against the doctrine of the cross because he thought it to be an imposition. His fault lay in his eyes, and so, when the eyes were set right, Saul was right. When he perceived that Jesus was, after all, the Messiah, the man became just as earnest a follower of Christ as before he had been a persecutor.

We will talk about scales falling from men's eyes. I want to address those who would be right if they knew how; who are earnest, but it is in the wrong direction, for they do not see the truth. If the Lord, in His infinite mercy, will but touch that sightless eyeball, and remove the film, so that they discern the right way, they will follow it at once. May the Lord remove many scales while we are proceeding!

This sermon was taken from *The Metropolitan Tabernacle Pulpit* and was preached at the Metropolitan Tabernacle, Newington.

First, we will speak of *scales which men fail to perceive, because they are inside.* Secondly, we will *show what makes these scales come to the outside so that men do perceive them;* then, thirdly, *what instrumentality the Lord uses to take these outside scales away;* and, fourthly, *what did Saul see when the scales were gone*?

There Are Scales Which Men Do Not Perceive

Saul had scales upon his eyes when he was on the road to Damascus, but if you had looked at his face he would have appeared to have as bright an eye as any man. Scales on his eyes! Why, he was a sharp-sighted philosopher, a Pharisee, and a teacher of others. He would not have believed you for a minute if you had said to him, "'Saul, you are blind." Yet blind he was, for his eyes were shut up with inside scales—the worst sort of scales that can possibly becloud the sight.

Saul had the scale of *self* to darken his eye. He had a great idea of Saul of Tarsus. If he had written down his own character, he would have begun it, "a Hebrew of the Hebrews; as touching the law, a Pharisee"; and then he would have gone on to tell of countless good works, and fastings, and prayers, and would have finished with, "concerning zeal, persecuting the church." He was far too great in his own estimation to become a disciple of Jesus Christ. How could the rabbi who sat at the feet of Gamaliel become a follower of the despised Galilean? Poor peasants might follow the Man of Nazareth, but Doctor Saul of Tarsus—a man so educated both in the knowledge of the Hebrew literature and of the Greek philosophy—it was not likely that he would mingle with fishermen and peasants in adoring the Nazarene. This is the reason why a great many people cannot see the beauties of Christ, and cannot come to Him that they might have life, namely, because they are so great in their own esteem. Ah, my lord, it might have been a good thing for you if you had been a pauper! Ah, good moralist, it might not be amiss for you if you would sit by the side of those who have lost character among men, and discover that, after all, there are not many shades of difference between you and them! Great "I" must fall before the great Savior will be seen. When a man becomes nothing in his own estimation, then Jesus Christ becomes everything to him—but not until then. Self is an effectual darkener of the windows of the soul. How can men see the Gospel while they see so much of themselves? With such a noble righteousness of their own to deck themselves with, is it likely that they will buy of Christ the fine white linen which is the righteousness of saints?

Another scale on Saul's inner eye was *ignorance*, and learned ignorance, too, which is by far the worst kind of ignorance. Saul knew everything but what he ought to have known; he was instructed in all other sorts of learning, but he did not know Christ. He had never studied the Lord's claim and character; he had picked up the popular rumors, and he had thought them to be sterling truth. Ah, had he known, poor soul, that Jesus of Nazareth really was the Christ, he would never have haled men and women to prison; but the scale of ignorance was ever his eyes. And how many there are, in this city of London, in what we call this "enlightened" nineteenth century, who know a great deal about a thousand things, but nothing about the one thing needful! They have never troubled to study that, and so, for lack of knowledge, they grope as the blind.

With ignorance generally goes another scale, namely, *prejudice.* The man who knows nothing about truth is usually the man who despises it most. He does not know, and does not want to know. "Don't tell me," he says, "don't tell me." He has nothing but a sneer for you when you have told him the truth to the best of your ability; the man has no candor, he has made up his mind, *he* has. Besides, his father before him was not of your religion, and do you think he is going to be a turncoat, and leave the old family faith? "Don't tell me," says he, "I don't want to know anything of your canting Methodism," or Presbyterianism, or whatever it is that he likes to call it. He is *so* wise! He is wiser than seven men that can render a reason. O prejudice, prejudice, prejudice, how many have you destroyed! Men who might have been wise have remained fools because they thought they were wise. Many judge what the Gospel *ought* to be, but do not actually inquire as to what it is. They do not come to the Bible to obtain their views of religion, but they open that Book to find texts to suit the opinions which they bring to it. They are not open to the honest force of truth, and therefore are not saved by it. Oh, that this scale would fall from every eye which it now closes!

Saul's soul was also darkened by the scale of *unbelief.* Saul had seen Stephen die. If he saw the martyr's heavenly face, he must have noticed the wondrous peace which sat upon his countenance when he fell asleep amid a shower of stones; but Saul did not believe. Though no sermon is like the sight of a martyrdom, yet Saul was not convinced. Perhaps he had heard about the Savior more than he cared to remember, but he did not believe it; he counted the things rumored concerning him to be idle tales, and cast them under his feet. O brothers and sisters, what multitudes are being ruined by this cruel unbelief toward Christ! Some of you, too, whom I have been addressing for years, are believers in the head, but unbelievers in the heart, not really putting your trust in Jesus. Who can see if he refuses the light? Who shall find salvation if he will not trust the Savior for it? Unbelief is as sure to destroy those who are guilty of it as faith is sure to save believers.

Then the scale of *habit,* too, had formed over Saul's inner eye, for he had been for a long time what he then was. "Can the Ethiopian change his skin, or the leopard his spots?" If so, then he that is accustomed to do evil may learn to do well. They say that use is second nature, and when the first nature is bad, the second nature is like the first, only it goes further in wrong. Ah, dear friends, some of you have been so accustomed to refuse the Gospel, so accustomed to follow after the pleasures and the vices of the world, that it does not seem possible that you should follow after Christ. Habits of secret sin are peculiarly blinding to the soul. May this scale be speedily made to fall!

Another scale is *worldliness*, and Saul had that upon his inner eye, for he loved the praise of men. He had his reputation to maintain, for he had profited beyond most of his brethren, and was reckoned to be a most hopeful and rising teacher of Israel. It was not likely that Saul would believe in Jesus Christ, for then he would have to lose the esteem of his countrymen. The fear of man, and the love of man's applause, how they prevent men from seeing the truth about Jesus, and recognizing Him as the Son of God! "How can ye believe, which receive honor one of another?" How can men bow themselves before Jesus Christ when, all the while, they are bidding high for the homage of their fellow-sinners? The love of adulation, which is a form of worldliness, blinds the eye, and so will any other love of things beneath the moon. Let but the heart be set upon this blinding world, and there will be little sight for things divine.

The Scales Are Brought to the Outside So Men Can Perceive Them

These scales were upon the inside of Saul's eyes when he was on the way to Damascus, but now we have to notice them brought to the outside. Those outside scales revealed in type and figure what had always been the matter with Saul; they were the material index of the spiritual mischief under which he had long labored, only now they were brought outside so that he knew they were there, and others could perceive that they were there. Now there was hope that they would be removed from the eyes; now that he was conscious of them, the evil was half cured. What brought those scales to the outside, and made Saul know that he was blind?

Well, first, it was *the exceeding glory of Christ*. Paul says, "About noon, suddenly there shone from heaven a great light round about me," and he adds, "I could not see for the glory of that light." Let my Lord Jesus Christ only manifest Himself to any of you, and you will be well enough aware of your blindness, and you will say to yourselves, "What a strangely blind being I must have been not to have loved such beauty as this—not to have yielded myself to such grace as this—not to have trusted myself to so complete a Savior as this!" Oh, the glory of Christ! It has even laid the saints prostrate when they have seen it. Those who dwell nearest to their Lord are frequently overcome with the exceeding brightness of His glory, and have to confess with those favored three—

> When, in ecstasy sublime,
> Tabor's glorious steep we climb,

> At the too-transporting light,
> Darkness rushes o'er our sight."

So it is with the sinner when he gets his first view of a glorious Christ, the inrush of the glory makes him mourn his native blindness; he perceives that he has had no perception, and knows that he has known nothing.

Another thing which made the scales pass to the outside of Saul's eyes was *that unanswerable question, "Why persecutest thou me?"* That brought home to him a sense of his sin. "Why?" That was a *why* for which Saul of Tarsus could not find a *because.* When he discovered that the Man of Nazareth was the glorious Christ of God, then, indeed, he was "confounded." He could make no reply to the demand, "Why persecutest thou me?" Oh, that the Lord would fix such a *why* in some of your hearts! Why should you live in sin? Why are you choosing the wages of unrighteousness? Why are you hardening your hearts against the Gospel? Why are you ridiculing it? Why do you sneer at the servants of God? If the Holy Spirit drives that *why* home to your heart, you will begin to say, "What a blind fool I am to have acted as I have done, to go kicking against the pricks, fighting against my best Friend, and pouring scorn on those whom I ought most of all to admire!" The *why* from the lips of Christ will show you your blindness.

The scales were on the outside of Saul's eyes now, because *his soul had been cast into a terrible bewilderment.* We read of him that, when his eyes were opened, he saw no man; but, trembling and astonished, he asked the Lord what he must do. Some of us know what that experience means. We have been brought under the hand of God until we have been utterly astonished—astonished at our Savior, astonished at our sin, astonished that there should be a hope remaining for us, astonished that we should have rejected that hope so long. With this amazement, there was mixed trembling lest, after all, the mercy should be too great for us, and the next word from the Lord should be, "You have kicked against the pricks so long that, henceforth, the gates of mercy are shut against you." May the Lord fill some of you with trembling and astonishment, and, if He does, then you will perceive the blindness of your soul, and cry for light.

I have no doubt the scales became all the more perceptible to poor Saul when he came to those *three days and nights of prayer*; for, when you get a man on his knees, and he begins crying for mercy, he is in the way of being more fully taught his need of it. If relief does not come at once, then the penitent cries more and more intensely; his heart all the while is aching more and more, and he perceives how blind he must have been to bring himself into such a condition. It is a good thing, sometimes, when the Lord keeps a man in prayer, pleading for the mercy, and pleading, and pleading, and pleading on and on, until he perceives how great his need of that mercy is. When he has bitterly felt the darkness of his soul, he will be exceedingly bold in bearing light to his fellowmen. May God bring many of you to agonizing prayer; and if that prayer should last days and nights, and you should neither eat nor drink for anguish of spirit, I warrant you that you will learn your blindness thoroughly, and the scales upon your eyes will be painfully evident to you.

What Instrumentality Did the Lord Use to Get the Scales Away?

Now, thirdly, and here I should like to stir up the people of God to a little practical business—we have seen Saul with the scales outside his eyes: he now knows that he is blind, though he did not know it before when he was a proud Pharisee. He can see a great deal better now than he could when he thought he could see, but, still, there he is, in darkness, and we long for the scales to be removed—what instrumentality did the Lord use to get the scales away?

It was not an angel, nor was it an apostle, but it was *a plain man*, named Ananias, who was the means of bringing sight to blind Saul. We do not know much about this useful brother. We know his name, and that is enough, but Ananias was the only person whom the Lord used in taking off the scales from this apostle's eyes. Dear brethren, dear sisters, too, there are some of you, if you be but alive to it, whom God will bless in like work. Perhaps this very night, though you are unknown and obscure Christian people, He may make you to be the means of taking the scales from the eyes of somebody who will be eminently useful in future years. The Holy Spirit blessed the great Apostle to the Gentiles by Ananias, and He may lead another of His mighties to Himself by some obscure disciple.

Ananias was a plain man, but he was *a good man*. You can see that Ananias was a thorough man of God. He was one who knew his Lord, and recognized His voice when He said to him, in a vision, "Ananias," and he was a man whom the Lord knew, for He called him by his name. "I have called thee by thy name: thou art mine." The Lord will not send you on His errands unless you are sound, and sincere, and living near to Him; but, if you be that, no matter how feeble you may be, I beseech you be looking out, even tonight, for some blind soul to whom you may be as eyes.

Notice, that this Ananias was *a ready man*, for when the Lord spoke to him, he said, "Behold, I am here, Lord." I know many professors who would have to answer, "Behold, I am anywhere else, Lord, but certainly not here." They are not "all there" when they are in Christ's work; the heart is away after something else. But, "Behold, I am here, Lord," is a grand thing for a believer to say when his Lord bids him seek the wanderer. It is well to say, "Behold, I am here, Lord, ready for the poor awakened one. If he wants a word of comfort, I am ready to say it to him; if he wants a word of direction, here am I, as You shall help me, to speak it to him." My brother, be like Ananias was, a ready man.

And he was *an understanding man*, for, when the Lord said to him concerning Saul, "Behold, he prayeth," he knew what that meant. He well understood the first indication of grace in the soul. Beloved, you must have a personal experience of the things of God, or you cannot help newborn souls. If you do not yourself know the marks of regeneration, you are useless.

At the same time, he was *a discerning man*—an inquiring, discriminating man, for he began to say, "Lord, I have heard by many of this man." He wanted to know a little about Saul, so he inquired of the great Master as to his character, and whether it was a genuine work of grace in his soul. It will not do to pat all people on the back, and give them comfort without examining into their state. Some of you must know by this time that indiscriminate consolation does more hurt than good. Certain classes need no consolation, but rather require reproof. They want wounding before they can be healed; and it is a good thing to know your man, and, especially, to wait upon the Lord, and ask Him to tell you about your man, so that you may know how to deal with him when you do come to him. Use all diligence to know the case, as Ananias did.

But when he had made his inquiry, he was *an obedient man*. He was told to go into a house where I do not suppose he had ever left his card in his life, but he did not stop for an introduction, but went off at once to the house of Judas, and inquired for one called Saul, of Tarsus. He had divine authority; the Lord had given him a search warrant, and so he entered the house.

> Thus the eternal mandate ran,
> Almighty grace, arrest that man.

Ananias must be the sheriff's officer to go and arrest Saul in the name of the Lord, and so away he went.

And you will notice what *a personal-dealing man* he was, for he did not stand at a distance, but, putting his hands on him, he said, "Brother Saul." Ah, that is the way to talk to people who are seeking the Lord: not to stand five miles off, and speak distantly, or preach condescendingly, as from the supreme heaven of a sanctified believer, down to the poor sinner mourning below. No, go and talk to him; call him brother. Go and speak to him with a true, loving, brotherly accent, as Ananias did, for he was *a brotherly man*.

Ananias also was *a man whose subject was Christ*. As soon as ever you do speak to the sinner, let the first thing you have to say be, "The Lord, *even Jesus*." Whatever you say next, begin with that, "Brother Saul, the Lord, even Jesus." Have something to say about Jesus, but say it personally and pointedly, not as though you were alluding to persons living in Australia seven hundred years ago, but as referring to Brother Saul, and intending the word for him.

Among Christian people, there are mighty hunters before the Lord, who strive after souls, but I wish a hundred times as many really cared for the souls of their fellowmen. Some church members never speak to anybody about spiritual things. You come into your pews, and you like two seats if you can get them; like gentlemen in a first-class carriage, you want a compartment to yourselves; and then, after service, no matter who is impressed, many of you have not a word to say. Should it be so, brethren? We should always be on the lookout to seat strangers comfortably, and afterward to drive home by personal remark any truth which may have been advanced. "Ah!" says one, but I may speak to the wrong person." Suppose you did, is it such a mighty misfortune to miss your mark once? Ah, brethren, if you were to address the wrong person fifty times, and ultimately meet the right one once in a year, it would well reward you. If you were to receive rebuffs, and rebuffs, and rebuffs, and yet at last you should find out the Brother Saul who is to have the scales removed by you, and by none but you, you would be well rewarded. A plain commonsense word from a commonsense Christian has often been the very thing to set some able critic at liberty. Some man of profound mind—a Thomas of abundant doubts and questions—has only just wanted a simple-hearted Christian man to say the right word, and he has entered into peace and liberty. You must not think that learned personages, when the Lord touches them in the heart, want to be talked to by doctors of divinity. Not they! They become as simple-hearted as others, and, like dying kings and dying bishops, they ask to hear a shepherd pray, because they find more savor, more plainness, more earnestness, more faith, and more familiarity with God, in the humble expressions of the lowly than in the language of courtly preachers. Do not, therefore, Brother Ananias, say, "I cannot go and talk to anybody. I have never been to college." Do not, sister in Christ, keep back because you are a woman, for oftentimes the Lord makes the sweet and gentle voice of woman to sound out the music of grace. God grant that many of us may be the instruments of taking the scales from men's eyes!

What Did Saul See When the Scales Were Gone?

The first person he saw was *Brother Ananias*. It was a fine sight for Saul to see Brother Ananias' Christian countenance beaming with love and joy. I fancy he was like one of our elders, a fine old Christian man, with love to souls written on his face. When Saul opened his eyes, it must have done him good to see just such a face as that—a plain, simple man, full of holy zeal and intense anxiety for his good. Dear friend, if the Lord opens your eyes, you will see the brotherhood of Christians. Perhaps you will enjoy that among the first delights of your Christian experience; and, for a little while, your faith, it may be, will hang upon the testimony of an instructed Christian woman, and your confidence will need confirmation by the witness of a more advanced brother in the Lord. But, my fellow-worker, the saved one will never see Brother Ananias unless Ananias goes to him, and becomes the means of opening his eyes; but if you will go and do that, you will win a friend who will love you as long as life lasts. There are some of you with whom I have ties which death cannot snap. I will find you out in heaven if I can, and I know you will desire to meet me. The Lord gave you to me as my spiritual children; and if it should come to pass that earthly fathers would not see their children in heaven, yet the spiritual father will see his children there praising and blessing the Lord. One of the next joys to knowing Christ yourself must surely be that of leading others to know Him. Seek after this bliss.

The next thing that Saul would see would be *a Savior in Christ*, for Ananias said to him, "The Lord, even Jesus, that appeared unto thee in the way as thou camest, hath sent me, that thou mightest receive thy sight." Now he would see what an opener of the eyes Jesus is, what a mighty Savior, as *my* Savior, opening *my* eyes, so that I can say, "One thing I know, whereas I was blind, now I see." This is a heavenly sight. May you help many to gaze upon it!

Speedily he saw *the Spirit of God waiting to fill him*: "that thou mightest receive thy sight, and be filled with the Holy Spirit." Ah, dear soul, when you have come to see Christ, then the blessed Spirit will become dear to you, and you will rejoice to think that He will dwell in you, to sanctify you, to enlighten you, to strengthen you, and to make you a vessel of mercy to others.

One more thing that Saul saw, when his eyes were opened, was what some do not see, although their eyes are opened in other aspects. "He received sight forthwith, and *arose, and was baptized*." He saw the duty of believers' baptism, and he attended to it directly. You who believe in Jesus should confess Jesus, and you who have confessed Jesus should gently bestir the memories of those very retiring young converts who are afraid to put on Christ in baptism. You know well that salvation lies in the believing, but still how singularly the two things are put together, "He that believeth and is baptized shall be saved." The two things are joined together by Christ, so let no man put them asunder. Surely, dear friends, wherever there is a genuine faith in Christ, there ought to be a speedy obedience to the other matter. I once met a man who had been forty years a Christian, and believed it to be his duty to be baptized; but when I spoke to him about it, he said, "He that believeth shall not make haste." After forty years' delay, he talked about not making haste. I quoted to him another passage: "I made haste, and delayed not to keep thy commandment," and showed him what the meaning of his misapplied passage was. Now, soul, do not delay. As soon as Saul's eyes were opened, straight way he took upon himself the outward badge of the Christian faith, and arose, and was baptized. Now,

I call upon you who love the Lord Jesus Christ not to play the coward, but come out, and own your Lord and Master. You that are truly His disciples, confess it. I like to see the soldier wearing his red coat; it is the right thing for him to wear his regimentals. It is the same with the soldiers of Christ. What are you ashamed of? Be ashamed of being ashamed, if you are ashamed of Christ. "Oh, but I am afraid I might not hold on my way!" Whose business is it to make you hold on your way? Is it not His business who has bidden you take up your cross, and follow Him, and who has said, "Whosoever shall confess me before men, him will I confess before my Father which is in heaven; but whosoever shall deny me before men, him will I also deny before my Father which is in heaven"?

I pray the Lord to bless these feeble words of mine. O souls, O souls, it does seem to me so dreadful that so many of you should come here continually, and yet be blinded! I try to talk plainly about your souls' need, and about Christ Jesus as able to meet that need; how long must I repeat the old story? Once again, I beseech you, think upon my Lord and Master, and see what a Savior He is, and how suitable He is for you. I would entreat you to delay no longer, but to close in with the invitations of His mercy. I think, sometimes, that my Master deserves that we should do more than invite you. We command you, in the name of Jesus of Nazareth, to bow before His scepter, for He is the King. Own His dominion, and let Him be your Savior; for this know—that His Gospel comes with divine authority as well as with gentle persuasion, neither can men reject it except at the peril of their souls. He whom I preach to you tonight will shortly come to be your Judge; and if you will not trust Him on His cross, you must tremble before Him on His throne. Oh, come to Him! Simple trust is the way to come to Him. Believe in Him, and He is yours, and His salvation is yours.

9

To Those Who Are "Almost Persuaded"

Then Agrippa said unto Paul, Almost thou persuadest me to be a Christian (Acts 26:28).

Notwithstanding his bonds, Paul is to be envied that he had an opportunity of addressing himself to kings and rulers, and that once at least in his life he stood before the great master of the Roman world, the Emperor himself. To reach the ignorant who sit on thrones is no mean feat for benevolence. Alas! the Gospel seldom climbs the high places of rank and dignity. It is a great act of mercy toward nobles and princes when they have the opportunity of hearing a faithful Gospel discourse. Highly favored was Edward VI to have such a preacher as Hugh Latimer, to tell him to his face the truth as it is in Jesus; and much favored was Agrippa, though he scarcely appreciated the privilege, to listen to so earnest an advocate of the Gospel of Jesus as Paul the apostle. We ought to pray much more than we do for men in high places because they have many bewitching temptations and less gracious opportunities than even the humblest paupers. There is less likelihood of the Gospel ever affecting their hearts than of its converting the poor and needy. We should make them therefore specially the subjects of supplication, and then we might hope to see consecrated coronets far more frequently.

Should a preacher be called to address himself to kings, he could not follow a better model than the apostle Paul whom we may fitly call the king of preachers, and the preacher to kings. His speech is extremely forcible, and yet exceedingly courteous. It is powerful in matter, but graceful in manner. It is bold, but remarkably unobtrusive; never cringing, but never impertinent.

This sermon was taken from *The Metropolitan Tabernacle Pulpit* and was preached on Sunday morning, May 16, 1869.

The apostle speaks much of himself for so his argument required, but still, nothing *for* himself, nor by way of self-commendation. The whole address is so adroitly shaped with such a sacred art, and yet with such a holy naturalness, that if any human persuasion could have converted Agrippa to the faith, the address of the Lord's prisoner was most likely to have done so. The line of argument was so suited to the prejudices and tastes of Agrippa as to be another instance of Paul's power to become "all things to all men."

Now it may be this morning, while we are speaking upon the apostle's teaching, and the results of it, that a great blessing may rest upon us, so that many of you may be persuaded to be Christians by the very arguments which failed with the Herodian king. Not many great men after the flesh, not many mighty are called, but this assembly is of another order, and, O may the Lord extend His sovereign grace along our ranks, through Jesus Christ our Lord.

The Great Object of the Christian Minister's Persuasions

Agrippa said, "Almost thou persuadest me *to be a Christian.*" I do not recollect a single sermon from this text that is fairly upon the words as they stand; they are all discourses upon being almost Christians, which, begging the pardon of the venerable divines, has nothing to do with the text, for the apostle never persuaded Agrippa to be almost a Christian; but he almost persuaded him to be a Christian altogether. Agrippa certainly never was an almost-Christian, his life and character displayed a spirit very far removed from that condition; he was not like the young man in the Gospel to whom the name "almost Christian" is far more applicable, although I gravely question its propriety in any case. There is a great difference between being almost a Christian and being almost persuaded to be a Christian. A man may be almost a Calvinist, and so may hold most of the doctrines of grace, but another who has been on a certain occasion almost persuaded to be a Calvinist, may be, as a matter of fact, a complete Arminian; a man who is almost an artist knows something of painting, but a man almost persuaded to be an artist may not even know the names of the colors. Now the great drift of Paul's preaching, according to Agrippa's confession, was to persuade him to be a Christian; and the apostle himself acknowledges the same design in his concluding sentence, "I would to God, that not only thou, but also all that hear me this day, were both almost and altogether such as I am." In that parting word of goodwill he unveiled the desire of his heart: he sought not release from his chains, but the deliverance of the souls of his hearers from the bondage of sin.

My brethren, the preaching of the Gospel minister should always have soulwinning for its object. Never should we seek that the audience should admire our excellency of speech. I have in my soul a thousand times cursed oratory, and wished that the arts of elocution had never been devised, or at least had never profaned the sanctuary of God; for often as I have listened with wonder to speech well conceived, and sentences aptly arranged, I have yet felt as though I could weep tears of blood that the time of the congregation on the Sabbath should be wasted by listening to wordy rhetoric, when what was wanted was a plain, urgent pleading with men's hearts and consciences. It is never worth a minister's while to go up his pulpit stairs to show his auditors that he is an adept in elocution. High-sounding words and flowery pauses are a mockery of man's spiritual needs. If a man desires to display his oratory, let him study for the bar, or enter Parliament, but let him not degrade the cross of Christ into a peg to hang his tawdry rags of speech upon. The cross is only lifted up aright when we can say, "Not with enticing words of man's wisdom, but in demonstration of the Spirit and of power." Every minister should be able to say with Paul, "Seeing then that we have such hope, we use great plainness of speech." No, my dear hearers, may it never be in any measure or degree an object of ours to flash and coruscate, and dazzle and astonish; but may we keep this one aim in view, namely, to persuade you to be Christians.

Neither would the apostle have been content if he could have persuaded Agrippa to take the name of a Christian, or to be baptized as a Christian. His object was that he might in very deed *be* a Christian. To seem is nothing, but *to be* is everything. I grant you that the apostle would have been glad enough to see Agrippa avowedly a Christian. Why should he not take the name if he had received the essential grace? He would have rejoiced to have baptized him. Why should he not, if he believed in Jesus? But the apostle was not anxious to confer misleading names. Nominal Christians he had no desire to create. To be or not to be was his great question; names and rites were secondary matters. It would not be worth the snap of a finger to Christianize a nation after the manner in which the zealous Francis Xavier made converts by sprinkling their heathen foreheads with a brush of holy water. It were scarce worth rising from one's bed to persuade an avowed son of Belial to put on the cloak of a religious profession and practice his vices in decorous secrecy. No, the persuasion of the apostle aims at Agrippa being a Christian indeed and of a truth. Thus should we labor in seeking converts; the adoption of a certain dress or mode of speech is little; union with our denomination is almost as unimportant; the true embracing of Jesus as the Savior of men is the vital matter. To bring men to be Christians, "this is the work, this the labor." The apostle does not appear to have aimed at merely making the man a convict as to his judgment, or a trembler as to his feelings, or an enthusiast as to his passions. Is it not sometimes evidently the drift of Christian ministers to make men weep for weeping's sake? Funeral rites are paraded, and sepulchers unveiled; mournful memories are awakened, and half-healed wounds ruthlessly rent open and this laceration of the natural feelings is supposed to be a process peculiarly conducive to conversion. I have no faith in such appeals; I want men's tears for other sorrows than those connected with the dead, I beg their heart's regard to a far more important occupation than garlanding the memorials of the departed. Is it not very possible to work up a congregation to the highest possible state of excitement upon their bereavements, and yet after all have gained no step in advance in the direction of their eternal salvation? The deaths of the Herod family might have been worked into a touching appeal to Agrippa, but Paul was too manly to attempt the sentimentalist's effeminate discoursings. Neither did the apostle excite Agrippa's patriotic sensibilities by rehearsing the glorious deeds of ancient Jewish valor with which the world had rung; no glowing stanzas of heroic verse or thrilling legend of chivalry were embossed upon his address, but in all simplicity the apostle aimed at this one thing: so far to convince the monarch's judgment as to change his heart, so far to affect his passions as by the power of the Holy Spirit to make a new man of him. This, this only, would content the apostolic orator, that his auditor might be a Christian, that he might be such a one as Paul also was, the Lord's servant, relying upon Christ's righteousness and living for Christ's glory.

Now, it is well for the preacher to know what he is at, and it is well for the hearers to know what the preacher desires to have them do or be. Why, brethren and sisters, I trust my heart's desire is precisely that which ruled the apostle. I long that every one of you may be a Christian. Ah, my Lord, I pray You bear me witness that the one thing I strive after is that this people may know Your truth and trust Your Son, and be saved by Your Holy Spirit: saved in their outward lives, and eternally saved in the day of Your appearing.

Whatever else shall come out of my preaching, though your liberality should be superabundant, though your morality should be untarnished, though your assemblings together should never decrease in numbers, though your enthusiasm should never abate in intensity, yet if you are not altogether Christians, made so by the new birth and by the power of the Holy Spirit, I shall regard my ministry as a miserable failure, a failure full of grief to me and of confusion to you. O may God grant that many here may be altogether and at once persuaded to be Christians, for nothing but this will content me.

If you desire a definition of a Christian, the apostle has given you it in the eighteenth verse of the chapter from which the text is selected. He there gives a fivefold description of the true Christian.

First, he is one whose eyes are opened, who has been turned from darkness to light—that is to say, he knows the truth of God, and perceives it in quite a different manner from any knowledge of it which he possessed in the past. He sees his sins and feels their heinousness; he knows the plan of salvation and rejoices in its all-sufficiency. His knowledge is not superficial, and a thing of the head, but internal, and a matter of the heart. He knows now truly what he only knew theoretically before. Knowledge is essential to a Christian; Romanism, that owl of night, may delight in ignorance, but true Christianity prays evermore for light. "The Lord is my light and my salvation"; light first and salvation afterward. May you all have the opened eye, which is the Spirit's early gift.

But the next point of the Christian is conversion, "To turn them from darkness to light, and from the power of Satan unto God." The Christian is emancipated from the tyranny of evil, and is free to follow after holiness, and to delight in the commands of God. He is a citizen of a new world, alienated from his former loves and desires, made a fellow citizen of a city with which he had no acquaintance aforetime. He owes no more service to the flesh and the lusts thereof but the Lord is his lawgiver and his King.

Thirdly, he has received forgiveness of sin. He is pardoned through the precious blood of Christ, and rejoices in the full remission of his sins. Faith has brought him to the cross foot, faith has led him to the fountain filled with blood, the Holy Spirit has applied the atonement, his conscience is clear; he has received redemption, to wit, the forgiveness of sins.

The next, and indeed the essential point in a Christian is faith: "By faith that is in me," says the Lord; faith in the crucified and risen Savior. From this root will spring all the other characteristics of the genuine Christian.

Once again, the Christian is a man who is sanctified—that is set apart, a separated man, a holy man, a sin-hating man, one who loves the commandments of God, and counts it his pleasure to be obedient to them. Such a man has salvation. He has already a part of the inheritance of saints, and he is on his way to that blessed place where he shall receive its full fruition.

It is after this that the Christian minister is always striving, that his hearers may be Christians—may be enlightened, may be converted, may have real and true faith; may be sanctified by the Spirit, may be forgiven all their sins, and may be made heirs of immortality. Has the ministry which you have attended effected under God this for you? If not, is this great failure the fault of the ministry or your own? O dear hearers, if the blame be in the ministry, if it be not such preaching as God will really bless, forsake it and attend some other! But if you are conscious that it is a Gospel ministry to which you have listened, because it has been blessed to others by the Holy Spirit, then I ask you, how will you answer for it at the bar of God, that so great a blessing of heaven has been slighted, and how will you excuse yourself for resisting cogent, earnest, affectionate persuasions, all intended to lead you to be a Christian? O confess your sin, that you still halt between two opinions, and remain in the gall of bitterness and in the bonds of iniquity, despite the pleadings of the word and the rebukes of your conscience. God grant that such inquiries may have the practical result of humbling and arousing you.

The Apostolic Manner of Persuading

Read carefully the notes of Paul's sermon as given in the chapter before us. In what way did he endeavor to persuade the king? I reply, it is note-worthy that Paul made *constant appeals to Scripture*. We say not that he quoted one or more passages, but he insisted from first to last that he spoke no other things than Moses and the prophets did write, and nothing but what the twelve tribes were looking for. My dear hearers, this ought always to be a powerful argument with you. You are as yet unconverted, you are not yet persuaded to be Christians, but yet you believe the Bible to be true. From your childhood you have accepted with reverence the Book of God as being inspired; now if this volume be of God, it is your highest wisdom to be a follower of Christ; and as you dare not reject the Book—you have not yet come to that pass—I ask you how you make it consistent with rea-son, how you reconcile it with conscience and with sound sense, that you remain disobedient to its high behests? That Book declares that no foun-dation can be laid for our eternal hopes but in Christ Jesus, and yet you have not built on that foundation! This Book testifies that those who reject the Lord Jesus and His atonement, must perish without mercy: are you pre-pared so to perish? It also invites you to build on the foundation of Christ's sacrificial work, and it promises you infinite security in so doing; are you willing to reject so great a boon? If you did not believe the Bible, no argu-ment drawn from it could have any force with you; hence the apostle did not quote Scripture to the philosophers on Mars' Hill; but granted that you accept the Scriptures as God's Word, as Agrippa did, the apostolic form of reasoning from that Word ought not merely to convince your judgments, but to persuade your hearts; and it would do so, if there were not something radically wrong in your hearts, something to be repented of, something to be removed by the power of God's Holy Spirit.

Observe next, the apostle's persuasion of Agrippa lay mainly in his *per-sonal testimony to the power of grace in his own soul*. We need not repeat the story of Paul on the road to Damascus, and the bright light and the sacred voice, and the sinner rising up converted to go forth to bear witness to others of Jesus and of His grace. Personal testimony ought always to weigh with men. Convince me that a man is honest, and then if he bears witness to facts which are matters of his own personal consciousness, not merely the gleanings of hearsay, but things which he has tasted and handled, I am bound to believe him; and especially if his testimony be backed up by others, I dare not deny it; I could not be so unjust. A great part of the preaching of every Christian minister should be in his bearing his personal testimony to what Christ has done for him. It was my privilege only last Thursday night to tell you over again for perhaps the thousandth time, how the grace of God has converted, consoled, supported, and benefited me. I did not hesitate to tell how the Holy Spirit led me to the foot of the cross, and by one look at the crucified Redeemer, banished all my guilty fears. I know I speak the truth, my conscience witnesses that I lie not, when I declare that trust in Jesus Christ has changed me so totally that I scarce know my former self; it has unbound my sackcloth and girded me with gladness; it has taken the ashes of sorrow from my head and anointed me with the oil of joy. Moreover, my testimony does not stand alone, but there are hundreds and thousands who consistently, and without hesitation, declare that faith in Christ has blessed and saved them. Such testimony ought to weigh with you, and it would convince you, were you not desperately set against the Lord's truth, and so fond of sin. Our testimony to the joy, peace, comfort, and strength, which faith in Jesus brings, ought to be accepted, being corroborated by the witness of thousands of men of undoubted truth and unblemished character. O that men were wise, and would not resist the counsel of God against themselves!

The apostle added to this twofold reasoning, *a clear statement of the facts of the Gospel.* Notice how he piles precious truths together, and compresses them as with an hydraulic press, in the twenty-third verse—"That Christ should suffer, and that he should be the first that should rise from the dead, and should show light unto the people, and to the Gentiles." He was about to complete this summary of Christian divinity, when Festus interrupted him. In that verse you have most of the grand truths of the Gospel. It is a ready way to convince men, so far as instrumentality can do it, to tell them clearly that God became incarnate in Christ Jesus; that the incarnate God bore the sin of believers, and suffered in man's place, that justice might be vindicated; that Jesus rose again, and ascended into heaven, to plead the cause of believers before the throne of God, and that pardon, free and full, is proclaimed to every sinner who will simply come and trust in the sufferings of Jesus. Where the Gospel statement is clearly given, even if no reasoning is used, it will, under God, frequently convince, for it is so marvelously self-evidencing; indeed, it would convince men universally, were not the human heart harder than the nether millstone, and carnal reason deaf as the adder that will not hear the wisest charmer.

The apostle did not close his sermon until he had made *a home appeal to Agrippa.* "King Agrippa," said he (in something like the style of Nathan when he said, "Thou art the man!") "King Agrippa, believest thou the prophets? I know that thou believest." He looked him through and through, and read his heart, and to escape that glance the king suddenly complimented him, and to avoid such close applications of unpalatable truth, withdrew from the place of hearing. Oh, but this is the way to preach! We must not only argue from the Scriptures, relate our experience, and give clear statements of Gospel truth, but we must also carry the war into the heart. The minister of Christ must know how to take the scaling ladder, and fix it against the wall of the conscience, and climb it sword in hand, to meet the man face to face in sacred duel for the capture of his heart. He must not flinch to tell the faults he knows, or to deal with the errors he perceives.

There must be a consecrated self-denial about the preacher, so that it matters not to him, even though he should draw down the wrath of his hearer upon his head; one thing he must aim at, that he may persuade him to be a Christian, and for this he must strike home, coming to close quarters, if perhaps by God's grace he may prick the man in his heart, slay his enmity, and bring him into captivity to Jesus.

Thus have I shown you the modes of persuasion which the apostle used, and the object for which he used them. O that such pleadings would persuade you!

The Differing Degrees of Success Attending Such Persuasions

How did Paul succeed? We can hardly expect to persuade more successfully than he, for we have neither his ability nor his apostolic authority. Note, then, that he failed with Festus, a rough soldier, an officer of decent character, one of the most respectable of the Roman governors who ruled Judea (as a whole a wretched band), an administrator of stern ready justice, very apt, according to Josephus, in the art of hunting down robbers, and generally a shrewd, vigorous, independent, but severe ruler of the province entrusted to him. He was the type of those commonsense, business people who are very practical, very just, very fond of facts, but who consider nothing to be worth their thoughts that has anything like sentiment in it, or that deals with abstract truth. "Thou art beside thyself," is the way in which Festus puts Paul down; and as if he noticed in Agrippa's face some little sympathy with the captive Jew, for the monarch's sake he tones down the roughness of his remark by adding, "Much learning hath made thee mad." The rough legionary neither knew nor cared much about learning himself, but he felt it a nuisance to be worried with Jewish cavils concerning rites and dogmas, and questions about one Jesus that was dead, whom Paul affirmed to be alive. He put such speculations all aside, saying to himself, "People who attach importance to such romantic speculations must assuredly be crazed or imbecile." Wherever the Gospel is preached there are people of that kind. "By all means," say they, "toleration—by all means; and if people like to believe this, or that, or the other, well—let them believe it. Of course, you know, we men of the world do not care a button about such matters—we know too much to commit ourselves to any set of dogmas; we have more practical and rational business to attend to." As to investigating the claims of truth, as to asking what is divinely revealed, as to giving themselves the trouble to study, no, no, no! Everlasting matters are by them (so wise are they) thought to be trifles. Time is everything; eternity is nothing! This transient life is all, the life everlasting is a thing to be sniffed at! Well, if such men bring grief to the preacher nowadays, he must not marvel, for such was Paul's burden in his day.

Now let us turn our gaze upon the young scion of the house of Herod, a man of very different mold. He listened attentively. He had always taken an interest in religious questions. He was sprung of a family that, with all their frightful vices, had trembled before the voice of prophecy and Scripture, and like the Herod who heard John gladly, he listened with great attention and interest to Paul. As he weighed the arguments in his mind, he felt that there was a great deal to be said for Paul's view of the question. He did not half know but what Paul might be right. Still he had an "if." He would rather not think that the prisoner before him was better informed than he, or that such stern teaching demanded obedience from him, and, therefore, he closed the discourse with a remark intended to be pleasing to the orator, and he went his way. Oh, but these Agrippas! these Agrippas! I would almost sooner deal with Festus, for I know what Festus means, and I am not disappointed; and one of these days it may be, the Lord will direct an arrow between the joints of Festus' harness; but this Agrippa utterly deceives me; he is a fair blossom that never knits, and so turns not to fruit; he is almost persuaded. Yes, and therefore he takes a sitting at our chapel, and he attends the ministry, and look, he even drops a tear, but then he would do the same if he sat in a smoky room. He will recollect what is said too, and when he hears a pungent remark he will repeat it at the dinner table, and commend the speaker, but then he would have done the same if he had been gratified by an actor at the theater. We are told that he is a good fellow, and well inclined! It may be so, but alas! he is almost persuaded and not quite, and so he is no Christian. He is not in any measure a Christian, although he listens to Christian preaching. He is almost persuaded, yet nothing more.

I wonder whether in Paul's congregation there was a third sort of hearer! I hope there was; for there were present not only Festus, and Bernice, and Agrippa, but doubtless many of the attendants, and certainly, according to the twenty-third verse of the twenty-fifth chapter, the chief captains and principal men of the city were there. Perhaps—though we are not so informed—while Paul was failing with Festus and disappointed with Agrippa, there sat somewhere in the back seats a centurion, or a private soldier, or a Jewish ruler, upon whom the truth was falling like soft dew, and into whose heart it was being received as the ocean absorbs the falling shower. Surely he was not left without witness: the seed he was casting on the waters was found again; and though he came up from his dungeon to preach on that occasion bearing precious seed with many tears, doubtless in heaven he rejoices over sheaves which sprang up from that morning's preaching. Blessed be God, our labor is not in vain in the Lord.

Why the Half-Convinced Hearer Was Only "Almost Persuaded"

Look at Agrippa again. Fix your attention fully upon him, for with some of you he is a photograph of yourselves. The arguments which Paul drew from Scripture and his own personal experience were very cogent; his way of putting these arguments was exceedingly forcible, and, therefore, if Agrippa were not altogether persuaded it was not the fault of the preacher's matter or manner. Nothing could have been more powerful in either case. Where, then, did the fault lie? I stand now in the court and I look around, and I ask myself "What is the reason why Agrippa is not persuaded? The argument tells on me, why not on him?" As I look around I notice on the right hand of Agrippa a very excellent reason why he is not convinced, for there sat Bernice, of whom there were very unsavory stories afloat in Josephus' day. She was Agrippa's sister, and is accused of having lived in incestuous intercourse with him. If so, with such a woman at his right hand, I marvel not that Paul's arguments did not fully persuade. The reason why sinners are not persuaded is, in ninety-nine cases out of a hundred, their sin—their love of sin! They see, but they will not see; for if they did see, they would have to tear out that right-eye sin or cut off that right-arm lust, and they cannot consent to that. Most of the arguments against the Gospel are bred in the filth of a corrupt life. He makes the best reasoner as an infidel who is most unholy, because the devil and his soul together will never keep him short of the fiery arrows of hell. If it were true that Agrippa lived in such degrading sin, it is no wonder that when Paul reasoned so soberly and so truthfully, Agrippa was almost, but not altogether, persuaded.

If the charge brought against Bernice as to her brother was not altogether true, yet she was beyond all question a shameless woman. She had been originally married to her own uncle, Herod, and was therefore both his niece and his wife; and her second marriage was soon broken by her unfaithfulness. Now Agrippa's public and ostentatious associating with her proved at least that he was in evil company. This is quite sufficient to account for his never being altogether persuaded to be a Christian. Evil company is one of Satan's great nets in which he holds his birds until the time shall come for their destruction. How many would rather escape, but they are afraid of those around them whom they count to be good fellows, and whose society has become necessary to their mirth! Oh! you know it, some of you, you know it; you have often trembled while I have told you of your sins and of the wrath to come, but you have met your bad companion at the door, or you have gone home and attended parties of gaiety, and every godly thought has been quenched, and you have gone back like a dog to his vomit, and like a sow that was washed to her wallowing in the mire. Ah, you Agrippas, your Bernices will lead you down to hell. But if Agrippa has his Bernice, Bernice has her Agrippa; and so men and women become mutual destroyers. The daughters of Eve and the sons of Adam assist each other choosing their own delusions.

Now that I am in the court, I look around again, and think I notice that Agrippa is easily influenced by Festus. Festus is a common sense rough-

and-ready governor, and such men always have power and influence over gentlemen of taste like Agrippa, for somehow the greater the diversity of character the more influence a man will have upon another. The rough Festus appears to the gentle Agrippa to be his superior, and if he sneers and calls Paul mad—well, Agrippa must not go the length of being persuaded, although he may demonstrate his expertness in Jewish questions by giving a favorable opinion on the case, which may a little put Festus down, yet how could he go and dine with the governor if he became quite convinced? What would Festus say? "Ah! two madmen! Is Agrippa also beside himself?" The king can hardly put up with the sarcasms which he foresees. Some people's sneers he could bear, but Festus is a man of shrewdness and commonsense, and is so prominent a ruler that a sneer from him would cut him to the quick. Alas, how many are influenced by fear of men! Oh, you cowards, will you be damned out of fear? Will you sooner let your souls perish than show your manhood by telling a poor mortal that you defy his scorn? Dare you not follow the right though all men in the world should call you to do the wrong? Oh, you cowards! You cowards! How you deserve to perish who have not soul enough to call your souls your own, but cower down before the sneers of fools! Play the man, I pray you, and ask God's grace to help you to do the right as soon as you are convinced, let Festus scoff as he will.

Do you not think, too, that Paul himself had something to do with Agrippa's not being convinced? I do not mean that Paul had one grain of blame in the case, but he wore decorations during his preaching which probably were not of a pleasing and convincing character to a man of Agrippa's taste for pomp and ease. Though better than golden ornaments were his chains, Paul seems to have perceived that Agrippa was shocked at Christianity in that peculiar garb, for he said, "Except these bonds." It often happens that looking abroad upon the sorrows of God's people, ungodly men refuse to take their portion with them. They find that righteous men are frequently sneered at, and called by nicknames. Their self-love can hardly run the risk of such inconvenience. Be a Methodist! No! Presbyterian! No! Truth is all very well, but gold, they say, can be bought too dearly. Men are so moved by the fear of contempt and poverty that they turn aside from the narrow path, and no reasoning can convince them to follow it, for they are unwilling to encounter the dangers of the heavenly pilgrimage. O that men were wise enough to see that suffering for Christ is honor, that loss for truth is gain, that the truest dignity rests in wearing the chain upon the arm rather than enduring the chain upon the soul.

After all, the great reason why Agrippa was not convinced lay in his own heart—partly in the love of pomp, partly in the dread of his master Nero at Rome, partly in his superficial and artificial character, but, mainly, in his love of sin, and in the struggling of his passions against the divine restraints of the Gospel. The main reason why men are not persuaded to be Christians lies in their own hearts. It is not a flaw in the preacher's logic; it is a flaw in the hearer's nature. It is no mistake in the syllogism; it is an error in the hearer's will. It is not that the reasonings are not powerful; it is that the man does not wish to feel their power, and so endeavors to elude them. I ask your consciences, you who are not convinced, whether I have not fairly stated some of the causes which create and prolong your halting between two opinions, and, if I have, may God's grace help you to confess them, and then may it deliver you from their power.

The Evil That Will Follow upon Being Only Almost Persuaded

The first evil is, that if a man is only almost convinced, *he misses altogether the blessing*, which the being fully persuaded to be a Christian would have bought him. A leaky ship went out to sea, and a passenger was almost persuaded not to trust his life in it, but he did so, and he perished. A bubble speculation was started in the city, and a merchant was almost persuaded not to have shares in it, but he bought the scrip, and his estate went down in the general shipwreck. A person exceedingly ill heard of a remedy reputed to be most effectual, and he was almost persuaded to take it, but he did not, and therefore the disease grew worse and worse. A man who proposed to go into a subterranean vault in the dark was almost persuaded to take a candle, but he did not, and therefore he stumbled and fell. You cannot have the blessing by being almost persuaded to have it. Your hunger cannot be appeased by almost eating, nor your thirst quenched by almost drinking. A culprit was almost saved from being hanged for a reprieve came five minutes after he was turned off, but alas! he was altogether dead, despite the almost escape. A man who has been almost persuaded to be saved will at the last be altogether damned; his being almost convinced will be of no conceivable service to him. This seems so grievous, that the life of God, and the light of God, and the heaven of God, should glide by some of you, and you should be almost persuaded, and yet should miss them, through not being Christians.

Worse still, in addition to the loss of the blessing, there certainly comes *an additional guilt* to the man who, the being almost persuaded, yet continues in his sin. A person has rebelled the government: in hot haste he has taken side with the rioters, but he is afterward very sorry for it, and he asks that he may be forgiven; let mercy have free course. But another offender has been reasoned with, he has been shown the impolicy of treason; he has seen clearly the evil of taking up arms against the commonwealth, and he has been almost persuaded to be loyal. I say when he becomes a rebel, he is a traitor with a vengeance, to whom no mercy can be shown. The man who is almost persuaded to be honest, and yet deliberately becomes a thief, is a rogue ingrain. The murderer who almost saves his victim's life in the moment of passion, pausing because almost persuaded to forego revenge, and, after all, deliberately kills his enemy, deserves death beyond all others. The man who is deliberately an enemy to Christ, presumptuously rejects the offer of peace, in calm moments puts from him the precious blood, who is almost persuaded, but yet by desperate effort overcomes his conscience, such a man shall go down to the pit with a millstone about his neck that shall sink him to the lowest hell. You almost persuaded ones, I pray you look at this and tremble.

Once more. To have been almost persuaded, and yet not to be a Christian, *will lead to endless regrets*; for will not this thought bubble up in the seething soul amidst its torments forever: "I was almost persuaded to repent: why did I go on in my sin? I was almost persuaded to put my trust in Jesus, wherefore did I cling still to my self-righteousness and vain ceremonies? I was almost persuaded to forsake my evil companions, and to become a servant of God, but I am now cast away forever, where no more persuasions can melt my heart.

"Oh, my cursed sin! Alas! that I should have been fascinated by its temporary sweetness, and for the sake of it should have incurred this never-ending bitterness! Oh, my madness! Oh, my insanity, that I should have chosen the lies which did but mock me, and suffered my Savior and His salvation to pass me by!" I dare not attempt to picture the remorse of spirits shut up in the cells of despair; suffice it to say, the dread truth is clear, a man cannot come so near to the verge of persuasion, and yet with desperate obstinacy start back from the great salvation, without incurring the hot displeasure of the God of mercy, without bringing upon himself also the doom of a suicide in having destroyed his own soul, and in having put from him the mercy of Jesus Christ.

How I wish I knew how to plead with you this morning! How earnestly I would persuade those of you who are halting between two opinions! Some of you have but a little time to be halting in; your waverings will soon be over, for your death warrants are signed, and the angel of death has spread his wings to the blast, to bring the fatal summons down. The grave is appointed for some of you within a few weeks or months. You shall not trifle with God long. O, I pray you, I beseech you, if you have any concern for yourselves, and have any sound reason left, seek that your peace may be made with God through the precious blood of Christ, that you may be ready to stand before your Maker's bar, for stand there you must and will, ere many days are past. If you should live another thirty or forty years, how short that time is, and how soon will it be past! Consider your ways now. Today is the accepted time, today is the day of salvation. The Lord persuade you. I have done my best. He can do it. The Lord the Holy Spirit create you anew and make you Christians, and His shall be the glory forever. Amen and Amen

10

A Sermon of Personal Testimony

For it is not a vain thing for you; because it is your life
(Deuteronomy 32:47).

These are among the last words of Moses before his death. He
addressed the people in a most tender and affectionate manner
before he went from them. "The old man eloquent" seemed as if he
would never leave off; he kept on reminding the children of Israel of the
goodness of God to them, and telling them what they might expect at His
hands if they would but serve Him. He pleaded with all earnestness again
and again, and at last used this master argument why he would have them
keep the ways of God, "for," said he, "it is not a vain thing for you"—it is
a most essential thing—"because it is your life."

It is very clear from this passage that there were some people, in the
days of Moses, who thought that it was a vain thing to serve the Lord; yet
those were very singular times, for if men rebelled against God, they were
smitten with sore sickness, and sometimes with sudden death. God was
then so manifestly in the midst of the camp that great miracles were often
wrought, and men were compelled to stand still and say, "This is the finger of God." Besides, whenever men in those days kept God's ways, they
prospered. That was the dispensation of temporal rewards and immediate
punishments; yet, though it was so, though the very bush in the desert
glowed with the glory of the Godhead, though the mountains smoked and
trembled beneath the touch of Deity, though the uplifted rod of Moses had
caused the Red Sea to be divided, and had fetched water out of the flinty
rock—yet even when Jehovah was so conspicuously with His people, there
were some among them who said, "It is a vain thing to serve the Lord."

This sermon was taken from *The Metropolitan Tabernacle Pulpit* and was
preached on Sunday evening, March 11, 1883.

This proves that miracles will not convince men if the Gospel of Jesus Christ does not; it also proves that, if God were to make His religion a thing of eyes and hands, to be looked upon and to be handled, it would still be rejected by ungodly men, for their hearts are set against it, and they are determined not to have God or Christ to rule over them.

Seeing that men thought it a vain thing to serve God in those olden times, I do not wonder that men would think the same now, for in these days, there are not such manifest judgments upon wicked men, neither are there always such apparent rewards for the godly as there were under the Mosaic dispensation. Nowadays, the righteous man is often sorely tried and troubled; sometimes he has more tribulation than his ungodly neighbors have, and his trials come even as the result of his serving God. On the other hand, does not the wicked man often prosper? Have we not seen him "spreading himself like a green bay tree," and covering the earth with his branches? This is the age of faith, in which God does not show Himself as He did in the old time; it is the dispensation of spiritual things, wherein spiritual men alone are cognizant of God's presence and working, and, therefore, it is no marvel that many turn upon the heel and say, "There is nothing in religion; it is a vain thing to serve the Lord."

Now, dear friends, I am not going to argue with you about this question, but I am going to bear my testimony concerning it. In a court of law, argument goes for much, but testimony is the thing which carries weight with the jury. They hear the evidence, and if they believe that the witnesses are honest and truthful men, they accept their testimony, and give a verdict accordingly. If they have reason to think that the witnesses are only acting a part, and speaking falsehood, they attach no importance to their evidence. I am going to give my testimony concerning the reality and blessedness of the religion of Jesus Christ our Lord, in the hope that it will convince some of you of the truth of my text, "It is not a vain thing for you; because it is your life."

I begin by admitting that there is a great deal of so-called religion that is a vain thing, and that is nobody's life. The religion of ceremonies is a vain thing. If any man shall tell me that, by any act of his whatsoever, he can convey grace to me, I shall not believe him. If he says that, by the application of water, he creates within an infant membership with Christ, and makes that child to be an inheritor of the kingdom of heaven, I shall not believe him. I shall attach no more importance to what he does, if he pretends to convey grace by it, than I should to the hocus-pocus of a gypsy, or the abracadabra of a magician. God does not convey His grace in that fashion, but by the working of His Spirit upon the mind, and will, and heart. True religion is not a thing that can be conveyed by water, or by bread and wine, apart from the state of mind and heart of the person receiving it. If my religion consists in putting on a certain dress, and showing myself as a mere performer, or in thinking that some good thing can come to the people by the sweetness of music, or the beauty of architecture, my religion is vain. It was not so with Christ and His apostles; they went everywhere preaching the Word, and proclaiming that "faith cometh by hearing, and hearing by the Word of God."

Then, again, a religion that consists in merely subscribing to a certain creed is a vain thing. Even if that creed were perfect, yet if your religion depended upon simply believing it as a creed, it would not affect you to any real purpose. Religion is a life grounded upon belief, but salvation comes not to a man simply because he is orthodox; if that is merely a matter of the head, and all the while the heart remains unaffected, and the actions are unchanged, such a religion is a vain thing.

I have also to admit, with very great pain, that there is no doubt that a large portion of the religion of the present day—the religion that consists in a mere profession—is vain. If any man comes to this place, and subscribes to the creed that I teach, if he be baptized with the baptism of Scripture itself, and if he be a most diligent man in all his devotions—yet, if he does not truly trust in Christ, if his heart is not renewed by the Spirit of God, if his life is not a life of temperance, chastity, holiness, and godliness, his religion is vain. It matters not that you are called Christians; the name to live is nothing, you must be spiritually alive. As our Lord told Nicodemus, "Ye must be born again." A man must be godly through and through, and when he is so, his religion is not vain.

It is to that religion I want now to bear my testimony as faithfully as I can: "for it is not a vain thing for you; because it is your life." I wish to give evidence in support of these four assertions; first, *it is no fiction*; secondly, *it is no trifle*; thirdly, *it is no folly*; fourthly, *it is no speculation*. May the Holy Spirit help me to speak and you to hear!

True Religion Is No Fiction

I speak on behalf of many who are present, and of an almost innumerable company who are not present, and who could not be present, when I bear witness that, having tried and tested the faith of the Lord Jesus Christ, we have not found it to be a fiction. We were told that there was God the Father, and we were bidden to address Him in prayer as our Father, and we have found that, "like as a father pitieth his children," so the Lord has pitied us, and loved us, and cared for us. We must always speak as we find, and we testify that, since the day we sought His face, all the love of the best earthly father has been eclipsed by the love of God which He has manifested toward us. God the Father a fiction? Why, in the lives of some of us, He is the greatest and most potent of all factors! We could do without anyone or anything else except our Father who is in heaven. We have often spoken with Him in prayer; and in His Word He has spoken back to us. In the time of trouble, it is our joy to run to Him, and cry,

"Father"; in our hours of need, He has supplied all our wants "according to his riches in glory by Christ Jesus." It is no use for any man to say that there is no such being as God, if he has never tried Him. There is no power in that kind of negative evidence. The Irish prisoner said to the judge, "There are three men who swear that they saw me kill the man, but I can bring fifty men to swear that they did not see me kill him." The judge soon exposed that fallacy, for there was no argument in it. If you say, "I do not know God, for I have never sought Him," we believe you, friend, and we believe you with the deepest grief, and we wish that you thought us as honest as you are yourself when we reply that we have sought God's face, and we are conscious, not by the sight of the eyes, or by the hearing of the ears, but by a new inward sense which God has given us, that in Him we live, and move, and have our being, and it is our joy to know that it is so.

Again, in the blessed Godhead, there is a second person, namely, Jesus Christ. Have we ever found Him to be real? It seems to be a current notion, even in the Christian church, that Jesus Christ is dead; but some of us believe in a living Christ, and well we may, for we went to Him all burdened with a sense of sin, and at the sight of Him upon the cross, our burden disappeared. And many another time have we gone to Him whenever that sense of sin has returned, and He has comforted us exceedingly with the abundance of His mercy. No Christ Jesus? Why, we have in secret had such fellowship with Him as a man has with his dearest friend, until we could doubt our own existence sooner than we could doubt the supernatural presence of Christ with true believers! It matters not if others say that it is not so with them; their sad experience does not prove how it is with us, and we bear our witness that, of all friends, the most real is Jesus of Nazareth; of all helpers and comforters, the truest and best we have ever found is Jesus Christ our Lord.

There yet remains another adorable person in the sacred Trinity—the Holy Spirit. Is there such a person? Does He work upon the hearts of men? I speak now, not for dozens or hundreds, but for thousands, and for tens and hundreds of thousands, when I say that He has new-made us; He has illuminated us; He has comforted us; He has strengthened us; He has guided us; He has sanctified us. He is with us, and we are conscious of His presence and His power. There are times when we are carried clean out of ourselves. We speak, you say, like men in a frenzy, though we are no more frenzied than you are. There are many of us who are no more fools than you are, and who could prove to you, in any matter of business or of science, that we are your equals in intellect, and we aver most certainly that there is a power beyond ourselves which has caused us to sing in the depths of sorrow, which has enabled us to rejoice when we have been racked with pain, which has made us sublimely calm when we have seemed to stand between the open jaws of death, and has carried us out of ourselves, so that we have freely forgiven those who did us wrong, and loved them all the better for their wrongdoing, and sought their good the more, inasmuch as they have sought our hurt. Such actions as these prove the presence and power of the Holy Spirit. He is no fiction to us, and to know the Father, the Son, and the Holy Spirit, is to some of us the most real thing that ever was upon the face of the earth.

I could wish that some who speak of godliness being all a fiction had known what I once knew when I felt *conviction of sin*. I think that I am usually as cheerful as most men, but there was a time when no poor wretch on earth was more sunken in despair than I was. I knew that, though but young, I had broken God's righteous law, and had grievously sinned against Him; under a sense of my guilt, I went about burdened day after day. If I slept, I dreamed of an angry God, and thought that He would cast me forever into hell. When I attended to my daily calling, the dreadful thought of my sin haunted and followed me wherever I went. If anyone had said to me then, "Sin is a fiction," I could not have laughed him to scorn, for I was in no laughing humor, but I could have sat down and wept to think that anyone should fancy that this grim reality was, after all, but a matter of foolish fear or craven dread.

Conviction of sin was real enough to me; so was *the joy of pardon*, for, one day, I heard it said, "Look unto me, and be ye saved, all the ends of the earth," and it was explained to me that Christ the Son of God did take my sin, and suffer for it, and that, if I trusted Him, I might know that He had made a full atonement for me, and that I was clear of all guilt. I believed that message, it seemed to come to me straight from heaven; I looked to Jesus and in a moment I leaped from the depths of despair to the heights of joyous confidence. I wanted to tell the assembled congregation that the witness of that humble preacher was true—that there was life in a look at the crucified One, and life at that moment for all who looked to Him. If anyone had said to me then, "That deliverance of yours is not real," I should have answered, "Let those who knew me only a week or two ago bear witness to the change it has wrought in me." As the sorrow was real, so was the joy real, too; the alteration wrought in me was so great that I hope it helped to make others see its reality by my life and conduct in endeavoring to serve God.

And since then—I am still bearing my own personal testimony—what reality there has been *in all spiritual things*, by way of consoling, and comforting, and strengthening, and guiding, and delivering! Religion not real? Well, some of us would willingly let everything else go so long as we may keep our faith. You may ridicule all we know, if you please, but you can never laugh us out of what we believe. If you had been in prison for six months, no one would ever convince you that imprisonment was not a real thing and if, on a sudden, you had been set at liberty, no one would make you believe that there was no difference between liberty and captivity, and that neither of those conditions existed. And, in like manner, we believe, and are sure, that there is such a thing as conviction of sin and pardon for sin, for both these things are to us matters of fact.

Mark, yet further, that religion is to us no fiction, for, since our conversion, we have received certain privileges which formerly we did not possess. I will mention only one, that is *the privilege of speaking with God in prayer*, with the assurance that He will answer us. Does God answer prayer? He who has never tried it is not able to tell, and it is most unphilosophical for any man to say that such a thing cannot be when he has never tested it himself; they who have tried and proved it are the ones who do know. I have sometimes wished that certain people could have seen some of the answers to prayer which I have received; I am sure they would have been surprised. Not long ago, a woman came to see me about joining the church. She was in great trouble, for her husband had gone away, under rather sad circumstances, to Australia, or somewhere in that part of the globe, and she could not hear any news of him. I said to her, "Well, let us pray for him." When I had prayed for his conversion, I prayed that he might come back to his wife, and I said to her, "Your husband will come back to you. I am persuaded that God has heard my prayer; so, when he returns, bring him to see me in this room." As she went out, she said to the friend who had come with her, "How very positively Mr. Spurgeon speaks about the Lord answering his prayer! He says that my husband will certainly come back to me." In a little over twelve months that woman was in my vestry *with her husband*. I had forgotten the circumstances until she recalled them to me. About the time of our prayer, God had met with him on the sea, while he was reading one of my sermons; as a penitent sinner, he was brought to the feet of Jesus, and he came back, and joined this church, and he is with us at this day in answer to that prayer. "Oh!" says someone, "that is merely a coincidence." Well, that woman did not think so, nor did her husband, nor did I at the time, and I do not think so now. You may call it a coincidence, if you like, but I call it an answer to prayer, and as long as I get such coincidences, I shall be perfectly satisfied to go on praying. "A rose by any other name would smell as sweet." I do not believe I would have had such coincidences if I had not asked for them, and as I get them daily, I shall stand to it, nor shall anything stop me from this glorying, that there is a God who hears prayer; I challenge all men to try for themselves whether it is not so. If they come humbly to God, by Christ Jesus, and seek His face they shall not seek in vain; and, by and by, if they continue to wait upon Him in prayer, He will gird them with power, so that they shall ask and receive both for themselves and for others.

Another thing I would like to mention that makes us feel that the religion of Christ is no fiction and that is *the many cases of conversion that are constantly witnessed among us*. If this were the time and place—and

I do not think that it is, for I do not care about such an exhibition of trophies of God's grace, and bringing men out one by one in such a fashion—I could tell, not alone of the drunkard made sober, but of the man, passionate and violent in temper, becoming as meek and gentle as a child. I could fetch him out from the congregation if you wanted to see him and I could point you to the swearer, who at one time found it impossible to speak without an oath, but who, from the moment of his conversion, was never again tried by that temptation. I could bring the thief who now knows what is his own, and what is his neighbor's, and who is honest as the day; and the unchaste, who were given up as if they never could be saved, who are now our sisters in Christ, and serving Him with modest, pure, simple hearts. Show us something else that makes such changes as these, if you can; show us something else, if you can, that will meet the needs of the hardened and abandoned people in the back slums. We do not know where to find it, but we do know that wherever Christ is faithfully preached such conversions are continually seen, and that morality and social order and everything that is pure and lovely are sustained and promoted by the Gospel of Jesus Christ wherever it is believed. These things are matters of fact; let those who care to do so resist the natural inference.

One of the strongest things which are no fiction is *the joy of believers when they die.* We have lately lost some of our dearest and best friends from the Tabernacle; some of our most earnest helpers have passed away, but, oh, they have died gloriously! It has been a pleasure and a privilege to see them rejoicing while everybody else was weeping—to hear them triumphant when all around them were sorrowful—to behold them casting gleams of sunlight from their eyes even when those eyes were being glazed in death. Give me a religion by which I can live, for that is the religion on which I can die. Give me that faith which will change me into the image of Christ, for then I need not be afraid to bear the image of death. God grant that you and I, dear friends, may know, as a matter of personal experience, that there is a solid truth in our religion, that it is indeed our life!

I know that there are some people who profess to disbelieve in religion altogether; yet, every now and then, they show that they do not doubt as much as they say they do. There was a traveler in the backwoods of America who put up one night at a log cabin. The man who lived in the house was a very rough-looking customer, and the traveler felt rather afraid of him; he had some money upon him, and he was half inclined to go walking on instead of stopping there. The master bade him come in, and eat with him; he did so, and after he had eaten, the man said, "Stranger, it is my custom always to read a chapter in the Bible, and to pray, before I turn in." The traveler said that in a moment he felt perfectly safe. He professed to be an infidel, but he showed that his infidelity was not very deep, for he believed in the man who worshiped his God, and was not afraid to sleep under his roof. William Hone, who wrote the *Every Day Book*, was an unbeliever once, but he was traveling through Wales, and he saw a little Welsh girl at the door reading her Bible. He said to her, "Ah, my lassie, you are getting your task, I see!" "What did you say, sir?" she asked. "I said that you are learning your task." "What do you mean, sir? I am reading my Bible; you don't call that a task, do you?" Well, he did think it was a task; it would have been one to him. She said, "Why, it is this reading my Bible that makes me happy all the day long! I am trying to learn some of it by heart, but that is no task to me, it is one of my greatest pleasures." And William Hone afterward confessed his own faith in the Lord Jesus Christ, to whom he had been guided by the joy that he saw in that girl's face. He could not help believing that there must be something real in religion after all; it was life to her, and very soon it became life to him also.

True Religion Is No Trifle

Godliness is no trifle, dear friends, because *it concerns the soul*. If a thing only concerns the body, I do not call it a trifle—cleanliness, temperance, obedience to the laws of health—these are very proper things to be urged upon men. I wish that people in general were more careful of their bodies; but the soul is immortal, it will live when the body shall have moldered into dust and ashes; therefore, trifle not with your souls. If you must play the fool, let it be with your moneybags. If you must speculate, let it be with your gold, but, I pray you, venture not upon any risk with your immortal spirit; make sure work for eternity: "for what shall it profit a man, if he shall gain the whole world, and lose his own soul?"

True religion also *concerns God*, and therefore it is not a trifling matter. If you must trifle with someone, trifle with your equal, even with your monarch, if you will; but never trifle with your God. He who made the heavens and the earth, and who holds all things in the hollow of His hand is to be worshiped and reverenced, but never to be trifled with. Beware, you that thus insult God, for trifling with Him will bring nothing but woe to you.

True religion also *concerns heaven and hell*, and these are not to be trifled with. True godliness is such a thing as no saint ever dares to trifle with. He strives to enter in at the narrow gate; he throws his whole energy into the running of the Christian race. No true minister ever trifles with the truth he proclaims. I have preached the Gospel now these thirty years and more, and some of you will scarcely believe it, but in my vestry behind that door, before I come to address the congregation in this Tabernacle, I tremble like an aspen leaf; and often, in coming down to this pulpit, have I felt my knees knock together—not that I am afraid of anyone of my hearers, but I am thinking of that account which I must render to God, whether I speak

His Word faithfully or not. On this service may hang the eternal destinies of many; O God, grant that we may all realize that this is a matter of the most solemn concern! May we all come to God by Christ Jesus, that everything may be right with us now, and right for eternity! God grant that it may be!

These are things which must not be trifled with, because their weight is incalculable; if we do trifle with them, there will be such damage as can never be remedied. A man who becomes a bankrupt once may start in business again, and yet grow rich. The commander who loses a battle may gather together his troops again, and yet lead them on to victory. But if the battle of this life be lost, woe worth the day! It is lost forever; there is no hope of any change to all eternity. It is not, therefore, a matter to be trifled with, but a thing to be attended to with all our might. I love to see Christian men in downright earnest. The other day, we lost a merchant from the city of London—a man of wealth and standing, and, at the same time, a deacon of a Baptist church. Just a night or two before he died, he was at a church meeting. He was unwell, and they could have done without him; but, as he was a deacon, he felt that he ought to be there. When his pastor said to him, "My dear sir, I think you should not be out," he answered, "If I had not been out today in Gresham Street, about my own business, I would not have been out tonight about my Master's business; but if I am well enough to look after my own affairs, I am surely well enough to attend to His." Let there always be with you, dear Christian people, this thought, that the Master's business must never be pushed behind your own, but that it must always be first and foremost with you: "It is not a vain thing for you; because it is your life." The highest point, the crown, the flower, the glory of your life, is your religion.

True Religion Is No Folly

First, *it is no folly to serve God*. Suppose, my brethren, it should turn out, after all, that there is no God. Suppose that we should all die like dogs, then there would be nobody left to laugh at me for having served my God; that is quite clear. I am of the same mind as Cicero, when he spoke about the soul being immortal, and someone said to him, "Philosophers will laugh at you for saying that." He replied, "They may laugh while I live; I am used to that kind of treatment. And if I am dead, and they also are dead, it is quite clear that no dead philosopher will be able to laugh at me." We who believe in Christ have two strings to our bow. If we live again in another world, all will be well with us. If we do not, we shall be as well off as you will be. We are as happy as you are, anyhow; we feel that we are far happier; so we are quite content to go on as we are. If it be folly to serve God, I am willing to be guilty of such folly as that. As I am His creature, I would serve my Creator; and as I am His child, I would serve my Father.

I think it is the chief end of my being to glorify Him here, and then to enjoy Him forever in glory.

Further, *is it folly to be reconciled to God?* Is it folly to believe that there is eternal justice, and that, if there be eternal justice, there will be a judgment; and that, if there be a judgment, there will be punishment for sin? Is that folly? And is it folly to believe that Jesus Christ came and bore the punishment for those who trust Him and that, if He bore that punishment, then those for whom He bore it may go clear; and that, if He bore it for those that believe in Him, then I, believing in Him, am clearly saved? Is that folly? It seems to me to be the most rational form of reasoning that I have ever come across yet, and to it will I stand. "God forbid that I should glory, save in the cross of our Lord Jesus Christ."

Next, *is it folly to be prepared to do your duty?* I venture to say that a man who is a true Christian is the readiest of any men that live to do his duty. I do not know whether it is ever a Christian's duty to kill people; but if a man be a soldier, it is wonderful how often religion makes him a better soldier. Read a bit of veritable history. An officer wanted to call out some troops in India for a certain duty, and he said, "At this time of night it is no use, for all the men are drunk, unless you send for Havelock's saints; they will be all right." And so they were. Some time after, it was rumored that one of the "saints" was drunk, and Havelock straightway made inquiry, and found that it was not one of his men, but another who bore the same name. The general said, "I do not know what Baptists are, but if Havelock's men are Baptists, I wish the whole army were Baptists, for there are no other soldiers like them." There was a commander who found his army better fitted for conflict because they feared the Lord, and lifted up their hearts in prayer to Him, and never turned aside to drunkenness and other evil ways. God grant that you, dear friends, may have a religion that will make you ready to do your duty, whatever it may be!

Besides, *is it not true wisdom to be prepared for your eternal destiny?* It is wise, some say, to look to present things; so it is, to a certain extent; but it is wise to look at present things in the light of the future. A man was dying—dying without hope, and without much concern, either, and his lawyer was called in to make his will. He was willing away all his property, and his wife and his little girl stood by his bed, and heard him giving his instructions. He said, "As to the home, you know, dear, I leave that to you"; so the lawyer put it down. His little girl said, "Then, Pa, you haven't got a home of your own where you are going." That sentence touched him; he had forgotten that matter; but, by God's grace, he was lead to seek and to find the home eternal. It must be a wise thing, not only to have a home of your own here, but to have another and a better home to go to when you die. A person said one day, "I know an infidel who lately died in perfect happiness and peace." "But," asked a workman who stood by, "was he in his senses?" "Yes," replied the speaker, "and he died in perfect peace." "Then," said the workman, "he must have had a very miserable time while he was alive." The other asked, "What do you mean?" He answered, "I will tell you what I mean. I have a very good, kind wife—the best woman that ever lived; and I have some dear children, too, and they are my comfort and joy; and if I had to leave them, and go away, I did not know where, and did not know whether I should live again or not, I would feel it the most awful thing in all the world to die; and I am sure that my wife would break her heart over it; but," he said, "now I can die in perfect peace because I feel that I am going home to my Father and to my Savior; and my wife can part with me in peace because she knows that I am going where I shall receive even greater love than she can give me. But I think that infidel must have had a scolding wife, and that was why he was glad to die; I cannot understand it on any other ground." No more can I; it looks to me to be a most unreasonable kind of composure for a man to lie down to die, and say, "I do not know where I am going; I expect I shall be annihilated." I shudder at the thought, I could not die like that. But when I know whom I have believed, and am persuaded that He is able to keep that which I have committed to Him, then I can with reason as well as with faith surrender myself into my heavenly Father's hands.

True Religion Is No Speculation

There are a great many speculations nowadays. If any of you want to lose your money, or are particularly anxious never to see it again, or want to have very limited view of it, I advise you to put in into a company. It will soon disappear; depend upon that. There are many speculations, and there are many people who become speculators; but there are some things that are certainties, and here is one. *If a man will trust himself with Jesus Christ, he shall be saved.* He may for some time be in darkness, but if he will fully trust himself with Christ, unless God can lie, and unless Christ can be defeated, such a man must and shall be saved, and he shall know it, too. There is not in hell a single man who can say that he trusted Christ, and yet that Christ did not save him; and I hardly think that there is anywhere on earth a man so base as to say that. At any rate, if he did say it, I would take leave not to believe what he said.

The process of salvation is very different in different cases. About two weeks ago, there stood in Cheapside a young man reading one of my sermons which had attracted his attention. As he was reading it, he came across this passage: "If you believe in the Lord Jesus Christ, you are saved now. But I want you to project your faith further, and to believe in Jesus Christ for the whole of your life; for if you do so, you shall not only be saved now, but you shall infallibly be saved forever." Than followed the text, "I give unto them eternal life," and this comment upon it: "Now, eternal life cannot come to an end. 'He that believeth on the Son hath ever lasting life.' Everlasting life cannot come to an end; it is a thing that lasts forever. Believe for everlasting life, and you have it, you are saved forever." The young man said, "Standing there, I did believe just as I was told. I trusted Christ, and I believed then that in Him I had everlasting life. The next minute, I felt, 'Oh, what a glorious thing this is! How I love Christ who has done this great thing for me! What is there that I can do to serve Him? What sin is there that I would not give up?' Then," said he, "I said to myself, as I walked on, 'Why, I am saved! I am sure I am, because now I love Christ; now I want to give up sin, and now I want to serve Him.'" And was not that a sure proof of his being saved, because he saw the greatness of divine love to him, and this made him grateful, and that gratitude turned him right round, and made a new man of him? This is how Christ can save you also.

Suppose you have been addicted to drunkenness, and that you are convinced of the evil of it. You go to Christ, and He forgives you; then you say, "Now I am forgiven, oh, how I love my Savior! I will never go back to my cups again; I have done with my old companions, I will go and seek out other people who love Christ, and I will join with them if they will have me; and I will see what Christ expects me to do, and I will do it, for I will do everything for Him who has done so much for me." That is salvation—a change of character—a deliverance from that which held you in bondage, an entrance into the blessed liberty of loving God and wanting to be holy. Oh, that we might each one of us know that blessedness! It is no speculation; you do not believe in Christ at haphazard. If you believe in Christ, heaven and earth shall pass away, but His Word shall never pass away; you are saved, as surely as God is God. He that believes in Christ shall be saved now, and in the hour of death, and at the day of judgment, and forever and ever.

Now, dear friends, in closing, I should like to say that *this salvation is suitable for all whom I am addressing*. Many of you know this, and you have been praying that others may know it, too. This salvation is suitable for poor men. If you are very poor, is it not time that you were rich toward God? And if you have the hard side of the hill in this world, why should you not have life eternal, and joy and bliss in the world to come? It is also equally suitable for the rich man, for if you have not somewhere to go when you die, I pity you. To leave your parks and gardens and mansions and estates, to go from Dives' table to Dives' hell, will be a horrible thing for you, my lord, and for your ladyship, if that should happen to be your case. You want a Savior, most certainly, rich as well as poor. This salvation exactly suits you, my aged friend over yonder. "Oh!" say you, "I am too fixed in my habits; I am afraid I never shall be saved; I am getting quite gray and very old." Well, then, this is the very thing to make you young.

"Ye must be born again." "Can a man be born again when he is old?" That is what Nicodemus asked, and Christ told him that he could be. He can put new life into you, so that you shall be a child even if you are a hundred years old; and you shall joy and rejoice in God that, in latter days, you have come to Him as a child, and received a Father's love. "Ah! but it won't suit me," says a young man; "I would like to see a little life." That is exactly what I want you to see, and you will never see life until you see Christ. "Oh, but I want to be happy!" you say. I know you do, and so do I; and I would like you to be happy. "I never believe in cats being cats before they are kittens; I like to see young people full of joy and full of merriment." I agree with you, but I tell you that there is more joy experienced by a Christian in five minutes than a by a worldling in five hundred years. When a saint lives near to God—

> His joys divinely grow,
>   Unspeakable like those above,
> And heaven begins below.

Talk of life and happiness, we have it who sought the Savior in our youth, and have never turned aside from Him since. This salvation suits everybody; it suits you, if you are a most moral person, and it will be your life. You are like a statue of marble now, very beautiful and fair to look upon, but you have no warm life of love to God within you. Oh, if we could only make that marble live!

> Oh, that those lips had language!

But the grace of God can put life into your dead morality. Perhaps I am speaking to some who are immoral; if that is your case, this salvation is just the thing for you. The religion of Jesus suits publicans and harlots; it is just the thing for the felon and the depraved. Someone here, perhaps, is half ashamed to be in this congregation; you are the very one I am sent after tonight—the lost sheep. It is you the Shepherd is seeking; He can afford to leave the ninety-and-nine that went not astray; but you lost sheep—you, lost woman, lost man—you are the very one that Jesus loves, for "the Son of man is come to seek and to save that which was lost." Come and cast yourself into His arms by simple trust, for that is faith. Trust Jesus, just as I lean my whole weight upon this rail; lean on Him your whole weight, fall flat down on His promise of pardon, lie right down on the rock; trust in nothing of your own, but trust Christ for everything, and you are saved. God grant that this may be the happy lot of us all, for Jesus Christ's sake! Amen.

11

Our Great Shepherd Finding the Sheep

Until he find it. . . . And when he hath found it. . . . And when he cometh home (Luke 15:4–6).

The love of Jesus, the Great Shepherd, is very *practical* and active. There is a sheep lost, and the Lord regrets it; but His love does not spend itself in regrets; He arises, and goes forth to seek and to save that which was lost. The love of Jesus Christ is love not in word only, but in deed and in truth. The love of Jesus is *prevenient*. He does not wait until the sheep is willing to return, or until it makes some attempt to come back; but no sooner is its lost estate known to the Shepherd than He starts off that He may find that which was lost. The love of Jesus to the lost sheep is *pre-eminent*. He leaves the ninety-and-nine in their pasturage and for a while forgets them, that all His heart, His eye, His strength may be given to the one that has gone astray. O sweet love of Christ, so practical, so pre-eminent, so prevenient! Let us ask for grace that we may imitate it, especially those of us who are called to be shepherds of men.

Among God's people most of the saints have a charge to watch over. However little the flock may be, even if it be restricted to our own family, or to the little class that gathers about us on the Sabbath, yet we are all our brother's keeper in some measure. Let us learn the love of Christ, that we may be wise in shepherdry. Let us not talk about our friends and say we love them, but let us show it by earnest, personal, speedy endeavors to do them good. Let us not wait until we see some goodness in them—until they seek after instruction.

> Oh, come, let us go and find them,
> In the paths of death they roam.

This sermon was taken from *The Metropolitan Tabernacle Pulpit* and was preached on Sunday evening, March 25, 1883.

And long before they have a thought of coming home, let us be on their track, eager to grasp them, if by any means we may save some. Oh, to have in our hearts such love of souls that it engrosses us so that we forget earthly needs, and only remember this yet higher necessity! It is a good house, said St. Bernard, in which Martha has to complain of Mary—where gracious pursuits put other work in the background. It is a choice crime that men should even grow lax about their lower business for a while, that they may devote their chief energy to the saving of the lost sheep.

Let that stand as an introduction. May we see the love of Jesus, as Bernard saw it, and we shall have had sermon enough.

In my text there are three periods to which I call your attention.

"Until He Find It"

Christ, the Good Shepherd, first will seek the lost sheep "until he find it." It is a long reach "until he find it." I like the expression. The Lord Jesus did not come down to earth to make an attempt to find men, but He came to do it, and He did it. He tarried here, seeking the lost sheep until He found it; He never gave over until His work was done. At this hour, in His work of grace among His chosen, He does not make an attempt at their salvation, and suffer defeat, but He keeps at soul-seeking work until He finds it.

Look at the seeking shepherd: he is looking for the sheep. Notice his anxious countenance until he finds it. We read that after he found it he rejoiced, but there is no rejoicing until he finds it. He is all excitement, quick of ear to catch the faintest sound, for it may be the bleating of his lost sheep. His eyes are like the eyes of eagles. He saw something stir in the bracken yonder, and he will be there in a bound or two; he is so eager. No: it was a mistake. It was not the sheep; perhaps it was some frightened fox. He climbs a hill, and from the top of it he looks all around. I was about to say that he looks with ears and eyes together. He puts his whole soul into the organs of watchfulness, if peradventure he may discern the sheep. Is there a smile on his face? Ah, no! not until he finds it. His whole soul is in his eyes and ears until he finds it. This is a faint yet true picture of that Great Shepherd who came here to seek His flock. So the evangelists have drawn Him in their pen-and-ink sketches of Him—always watchful; spending night and day in prayers, and tears, and entreaties; never more to have a joy until He find the lost one. Then, when He did find a single sheep, finding His meat and His drink in it, and becoming refreshed from the fact that He has so far accomplished His beloved work. The Great Shepherd is all energy, care, and concentration of thought concerning His sheep, "until he find it."

Like the shepherd, there is no hesitating with Jesus. The sheep is lost, and the news is brought to the shepherd; he girds his loose robe about him, and is on the way. He knows within a little which way that stray sheep will go, and he is on its track at once, though he knows that he must mark that track with his blood. See the blessed shepherd pressing on: there is no pausing nor resting until he finds it. He has made up his mind that no sheep of his shall be lost, and he hies over hill and dale after the wanderer until he find it.

If you look into that shepherd's face, there is no trace of anger there. He does not say, "Oh, that I should be worried with this silly sheep thus going astray!" No thought is there but that of anxious love. It is all love, and nothing else but love, before he finds and until he finds it; and you may be sure that careful tenderness will be in full action after he has found it. He is looking with anxious eye of love. "As I live," says the Lord, "I have no pleasure in the death of him that dieth, but that he should turn unto me and live." "Until he find it" there will be no thought of anxiety, but a fullness of pitying care for the lost sheep.

And, mark, for a shepherd there is no giving up. That sheep has wandered now for many hours. The sun has risen, and the sun has set; or, at least it is just going down; but as long as the shepherd can see, and the sheep is still alive, he will pursue it "until he find it." He has been disappointed a great many times; and when he thought that he should have found it, he has missed it; but still, he will never give up. He is impelled onward by irresistible love, and he must continue his weary search until he find it. It was precisely so with our Lord Jesus Christ. When He came after you and after me, we ran from Him, but He pursued us: we hid from Him, but He discovered

He had almost grasped us, but so long as we eluded Him He still pursued with love unwearied until He found us. Oh, if He had given up after the first ten years—if He had ceased to care for some of us after fifty different occasions in which we had choked conscience and quenched the Spirit, then we should have been lost. But He would not be turned away. If He determines to save, He continues to pursue the rambling sheep until He finds it. He cannot, He must not, He will not, cease from the work of seeking and of finding until He finds it. I wish tonight that the time were come with some here that it would be said, "The Savior did pursue such and such a one until He found him—found him in the Tabernacle, and ended all his wanderings there—found him standing in yonder gallery, and ended all his wanderings at the foot of the cross." God grant that it may be so! But whether it be so with you or not, be sure of this—that the Lord Jesus has in hundreds and thousands of cases pursued sinners with unflagging mercy, leaping to them over hills of sin, and following them until He has found them. We are now His forever and ever, for He who has found us will never lose us. Blessed be His name!

Learn this lesson before I pass on. If ever you are seeking the conversion of any man follow him up until you find him. Do not be discouraged. Put up with a great many rebuffs and rebukes; you will have him yet. He is surest to succeed who cannot be put off from his aim. From some it will be necessary to receive a great deal that is most discouraging. Receive it, and say nothing about it; only whisper to yourself, "I might well have put the Great Shepherd off from caring for me, and yet He was not so turned aside. If He persevered with me even to the death, I may well persevere as long as I live in seeking and finding a soul." I have heard of wives who have pleaded with God for their husbands twenty years, and yet have seen them converted after all. There are instances in this place in which indefatigable love has followed up ungodly relatives until they have at last been saved by sovereign grace. Persevere with loving entreaties! Until you bury your unsaved ones, do not consider them dead; do not bury them spiritually until they are dead really. Some are easily baffled. They have written the death warrant of a friend by ceasing to pray for him, and yet that death warrant will never be written in the records of heaven, for the friend will be brought to the Savior's feet.

"Until he find it." Now nail your colors to the mast. "Until he find it." Go out, under-shepherds for Christ. Wear this motto on your right hand, "Until I find it." Live or die, or work or suffer, whether the time be short or long, or the way be smooth or rough, let each one of you be bound to seek a soul "until he find it." You will find it then, even as Christ found you.

"And When He Hath Found It"

When the shepherd has found the sheep, what does he do then? Well, first, *he takes fast hold*. "He layeth it on his shoulders rejoicing." So when he has found it, the first thing is to get a tight grip of it. See him: he has got close up to the sheep. The poor thing is spent, and yet may have strength enough to get away, therefore the shepherd takes good care that he shall not. He grasps its legs and holds it tight. That is what the Lord Jesus does when at last He gets a man broken down under a sense of sin, spent and worn out as to further resistance of divine mercy. Our Lord gets such a grip of the rebel that he will never get away any more. I remember when He laid hold of me. He has never lost His grasp even to this day. But, oh, it was a grasp! Nothing ever gripped my fickle mind like the hand of Christ. When the divine hand, which fixed the foundations of the earth, had fixed itself on me, my wanderings were ended once for all.

The next thing after the fast hold was *the gracious lift*. He lifted this poor sheep up and put it on his shoulders, and there it was with all its weight, carried by powerful shoulders. That is what the Savior does for poor weary sinners. He carries the weight of their sin, nay the weight of themselves. He takes us just as we are, and instead of driving us back by His law, He carries us home by His love. Instead of urging us to go home, He becomes the great burden bearer of His redeemed, and bears them on His shoulders. And now you have before you one of the loveliest of portraits that ever imagination can sketch—that great crowned Shepherd of the sheep, King of Kings and Lord of Lords, bearing on His shoulders, as a burden He delights to carry, the sheep that had gone astray. Oh, I pray God that you may be on those broad shoulders if you never have been so favored. The shoulders of omnipotence bearing up our weakness—the mighty Savior bearing us and all our sin and all our care, and our whole beings upon the shoulders of His strength—this is a sight for angels.

And as He thus carries the weight, observe that *the distance is removed*. We read in the next verse, "When he cometh home," but there is nothing said about the road, for somehow our Master has the knack of being at home at once. The sinner may weary himself by twenty years of sin, but in five minutes that may all be gone. It may have taken you fifty years to make yourself such a hell-deserving sinner as you are, but it will not take Jesus fifty ticks of the clock to wash you and make you whiter than snow, and to get you back into the great Father's house. Truth to tell, the Shepherd's redeeming work is done already.

> How dreadful was the hour,
> When God our wanderings laid,
> And did at once his vengeance pour
> Upon our Shepherd's head!
>
> How glorious was the grace,
> When Christ sustained the stroke!
> His life and blood the Shepherd pays,
> A ransom for the flock.

By that redeeming process He brought us near to God.

There is no weary journey back for shepherd or sheep. He grasps the sheep; he puts it on his shoulders, and they are both back at the fold.

But the particular point I want you to notice is when the shepherd gets this burden on his back. We read, "When he hath found it he layeth it upon his shoulders"—with great anxiety? Look to see whether it is so. Nothing of the sort. But is it not, "He layeth it on his shoulders with great weariness"? No. See! See! "He layeth it on his shoulders rejoicing"—*rejoicing*. He does not remember all the weariness that he has had to suffer. He does not think of the folly of his sheep in having lost good pasture, in having involved itself in so much danger, and in costing him so much labor. Not a word is mentioned of it. "He layeth it on his shoulders rejoicing." He says to himself, "I am glad to carry this burden, happy to carry my lost sheep home." And oh! I do love to picture to myself at this moment the joy in the heart of the blessed Christ. "For the joy that was set before him he endured the cross, despising the shame." And now, whenever He gets a lost sheep to carry back—He rejoices. His heart leaps within Him. All anxiety is gone. Fullness of delight is upon Him. "He layeth it upon his shoulders rejoicing."

I wonder whether the sheep could see that the shepherd rejoiced. I do not suppose that it could; but it could feel it. There are two ways, you know, of handling a sheep, and the sheep very soon knows which expresses pleasure on its owner's part. If you speak angrily to a sheep, and throw it upon your shoulder with indignation, that is one thing; but if you have not a word to say, except it be, "Poor thing, I am glad I have found you," and you cast it on your shoulders rejoicing, why, sheep as it is, it knows the difference. At any rate, I know that Christ has a way of saving us: oh, so gently, so lovingly, so gleefully, that He makes us happy in being saved. There is a way of turning a dollar into stone or into gold according to the way in which you give it to a poor man. You can fling it at him as if he were a dog, and he will be about as grateful to you as a dog, or not so much. But there is a way in which you can say, "I am sorry for your needs. This is all I can afford you now. Take it, and do what you can with it." Given with a brotherly look, it will be gratefully received, and made the most of. There is much in the manner, as well as in the matter of a gift. The mannerism of Christ is grandly gracious: He saves us rejoicingly. It is a matter of thanksgiving to Him when He gets hold of His lost sheep, and gets it on His shoulders. It makes me glad to think that it is so.

We are not saved by a grudging Christ, who seems as if He were weary of us, and must save us out of hand, to get rid of us. He does not act with us as some rude surgeon might do who says, "I will attend to you directly, but I have plenty else to do, and you *gratis* patients are a trouble." Nor does He roughly set the bone. No; Jesus comes, and He molds the dislocated joint, and when He sets it—there is bliss even about the method of the setting. We look into His face, and we see that He puts His most tender sympathy into each movement. You know the different ways which workmen have. Some kind of work a man is soon sick of. The principle of division of labor is a very admirable one for the production of results upon a large scale, but it is a miserable business for the workman to have to do the same thing over and over again, all day long, as if he were an automaton. Get a man at work at a statue—an artist whose whole soul is in his chisel, who knows that there is a bright spirit within that block of marble, and who means to chip off all that hides the lovely image from his sight. See how he works! No man does a thing well who does it sorrowfully. The best work that can be is done by the happy, joyful workman, and so it is with Christ. He does not save souls as of necessity—as though He would rather do something else if He might; but His very heart is in it, He rejoices to do it, and therefore He does it thoroughly, and He communicates His joy to us in the doing of it.

Now, learn a lesson before I go away to the third point. "When he hath found it." Suppose that any of you should very soon meet with a poor troubled sinner, anxious to come to Christ. When you have found him, let me recommend you to imitate the Master's example: get a tight grip of him. Do not let him slip. Get a hold of him; and then, if he is in trouble, take all that trouble upon yourself. Try whether you cannot get him upon your shoulders. Imitate your Master in that way. Try to bear all his burden for him, as Christ bore yours. Conduct him to the Christ who is the true burden bearer; and all the while be very happy about it. I do not think we ought to go and talk to young converts in a dreadfully solemn tone, as though it would be something horrible to find a Savior. They will never come again, you may depend upon it. They will give you a wide berth. But just go, and in a joyful spirit say, "I am so glad to find you caring about your soul." The best thing that can happen to a soul-seeker is to meet with a troubled conscience; show that you think so. "But," say you, "I have not the time." Always have time, even in the middle of the night, to see a poor conscience-stricken sinner. But perhaps you are very weary, or not well. If I were weary I should not be weary any longer when I came across a lost sheep; and if I were ill, I would get well on purpose to see after a sin-sick sinner. Talk in that way, with sweet and pleasant encouragement, for this is the way to help your brother sinner to the Savior.

My time has gone, but just a few words more on this last point.

"When He Cometh Home"

"When he cometh home, he calleth together his friends and neighbors, saying unto them, Rejoice with me; for I have found my sheep which was lost."

Some hurried observations. First, *heaven is a home.* "When he cometh home," and the next verse says that it is heaven. Heaven is a home. Do you not like to think of it under that aspect? It is the home of Jesus, and if it is the home of Jesus can any other home be equal to it? "When he cometh home."

Note that *lost ones are known in heaven.* I give you that thought more from the Greek than from the English here. "When he comes home, he calls together his friends and neighbors, saying to them, Rejoice with me; for I have found my sheep—the lost one." That is how it should run. It is as if the friends knew that one had been lost, and the loss had been deplored, and the shepherd says, "I have found my sheep; you know which one—the lost one." Up there they know which are Christ's sheep, and which are lost. Heaven is nearer earth than some of us dream. How long does it take to get there?

> One gentle sigh the spirit breaks:
>   We scarce can say, "He's gone,"
> Before the ransomed spirit takes
>   Its mansion near the throne.

And there are more communications between earth and heaven than some folk dream; for here it is clear that when the shepherd came home he said to them, "I have found the sheep," the lost one. So they knew all about it. It is evident, again, that they all knew there that the shepherd had gone after the sheep, for he says, "I have found my sheep which was lost." They all knew that he had gone on search, and therefore they could all understand his joy when he came back with the sheep. I believe that they know in heaven when Christ is seeking after anyone. It must be a great satisfaction to some up there who die with an unconverted son, or an unconverted daughter, to know, after a little while, son or daughter is converted to Christ. I am persuaded they know it. They cannot help knowing it, because they are Christ's friends and neighbors, and, according to the parable, He tells them, and He says to them, "Rejoice with me"; and if He says, "Rejoice with me," why, of course, He tells them why. You don't think that Jesus ever invited a spirit before the throne to rejoice with Him, and received for answer, "I cannot do it, for I know no cause for joy." If I had been converted after my mother's death, I can fancy that when Jesus said to all of them, "Rejoice with Me, for I have found My sheep, the lost one," my mother would say, "My Lord, I can rejoice more than any of them, for that was my boy, and he is saved at last." Your mother in glory will be twice glorified tonight, John, if you give your heart to Christ, and I pray that you may. Your father, now before the throne, will think that paradise has grown more paradisiac than ever if he hears it whispered down the golden streets that the wanderer has come home.

Notice that *Jesus Christ loves other people to rejoice with Him*, so that, when He finds a sinner, He has so much love in His heart that His joy runs over, and He cries to others, "Come, friends, come neighbors, come and help me to be glad, for I have saved another soul." Let us catch the blessed infection. If you have just heard of somebody being saved, be glad about it. Though you do not know the person, yet be glad about it, because Jesus is glad.

Notice, next, that *repentance is regarded as coming home*. This sheep was not in heaven. No, but as soon as it had been brought into the fold it is described as repenting, and Jesus and the angels begin to rejoice over it. If a man truly repents, and Christ saves him, it is clear that he never will be lost. A certain old proverb forbids us to count our chickens until they are hatched, and I do not think that angels would do so in the case of immortal souls. If they believed that repenting sinners might afterward be lost, they would not ring the marriage bells just yet, but they would wait a while to see how things went on. If they can yet perish there is not one convert that the angels dare rejoice over, for if any child of God might fall away and perish, why not every one of us? If any one falls from grace, I fear I shall. O my brother, do you not fear the same for yourself? "No," say you, "I don't think so." Well, then, you are a proud fellow, and you are the most likely one to desert your Lord. If ever a sheep of Christ's shall fall away, I shall. I see more of my own tendencies to wander, and more of my own temptations to offend than I do of yours. I would not have the angels rejoice over a man because he repents, if repentance be only a sign of human improvement, and not a token of heavenly love. I would say, "Stop, angels, for this man may go back, and perish after all, if, according to the modern Gospel Christ loves today and hates tomorrow, and a child of God may yet be a child of the devil." I do not believe a word of such doctrine. I believe that where the Lord begins the good work of grace He will carry it on, and perfect it; and when the Lord has once given to a man to know Him, He will see that he is preserved in that knowledge forever. There is a text that clenches it: "I give unto my sheep eternal life, and they shall never perish, neither shall any man pluck them out of my hand." Now, if they have eternal life, it cannot come to an end, for eternal life is eternal, evidently; if they have eternal life, the Shepherd and His friends may justifiably sing when one single possessor of that eternal life is brought to life and salvation. In the penitent man a work is done that never can be undone, and he is put where he never can be lost. Yes,

> I to the end shall endure,
> As sure as the earnest is given;
> More happy, but not more secure,
> Are the glorified spirits in heaven.

Sing away, angels! There is something to sing about now, and we will join with you in blessing and praising the unchanging God forever and forever. Amen.

12

Travailing for Souls

As soon as Zion travailed, she brought forth her children (Isaiah 66:8).

I srael had fallen into the lowest condition, but an inward yearning of heart was felt in the midst of God's people for the return of the divine blessing; no sooner had this anxious desire become intense than God heard the voice of its cry, and the blessing came. It was so at the time of the restoration of the captives from Babylon, and it was most evidently so in the days of our Lord. A faithful company had continued still to expect the coming of the Lord's anointed messenger; they waited until he should suddenly come in his temple; the twelve tribes represented by an elect remnant cried day and night to the Most High, and when at last their prayers reached the fullness of vehemence, and their anxiety wrought in them the deepest agony of spirit, then the Messiah came: the light of the Gentiles, and the glory of Israel. Then began that age of blessedness in which the barren woman did keep house and became the joyful mother of children. The Holy Spirit was given, and multitudes were born to the church of God, yes, we may say, a nation was born in a day. The wilderness and the solitary place were glad for them, and the desert rejoiced and blossomed as the rose. We are not, however, about to enter into the particular application of our text as Isaiah uttered it; the great declarations of revelation are applicable to all cases, and, once true, they stand fast forever and ever. Earnestly desiring that God may give a large spiritual blessing to His church this morning through the subject to which my mind has been directed, I shall first ask you to note that *in order to the obtaining of an increase to the church there must be travail*; and that, secondly, *this travail is frequently followed by surprising results*. I shall then have to show why *both the travail and the result are desirable*, and pronounce *woe on*

This sermon was taken from *The Metropolitan Tabernacle Pulpit* and was preached on Sunday morning, September 3, 1871.

those who stand back and hinder it, and *a blessing on such as shall be moved by God's own Spirit to travail for souls.*

There Must Be Travail to Obtain an Increase to the Church

It is clear from the text, "As soon as Zion travailed, she brought forth her children," that there must be the travail before there will be the spiritual birth.

Let me first *establish this fact from history.* Before there has fallen a great benediction upon God's people, it has been preceded by great searchings of heart. Israel was so oppressed in Egypt that it would have been a very easy and almost a natural thing for the people to become so utterly crushed in spirit as to submit to be hereditary bondslaves, making the best they could of their miserable lot, but God would not have it so; He meant to bring then out "with a high hand and an outstretched arm." Before, however, He began to work He made them begin to cry. Their sighs and cries came up into the ears of God, and He stretched out His hand to deliver them. Doubtless, many a heartrending appeal was made to heaven by mothers when their babes were torn from their breasts to be cast into the river. With what bitterness did they ask God to look on His poor people Israel, and avenge them of their oppressors. The young men bowed under the cruel yoke and groaned, while hoary sires, smarting under ignominious lashes from the taskmaster, sighed and wept before the God of Israel. The whole nation cried, "O God visit us; God of Abraham, of Isaac, and of Jacob, remember thy covenant, and deliver us." This travail brought its result, for the Lord smote the field of Zoan with mighty plagues, and forth from under the bondage of the sons of Misraim the children of Israel marched with joy.

As we shall not have time to narrate many instances, let us take a long leap in history to the days of David. The era of the son of Jesse was evidently a time of religious revival. God was honored and His service maintained in the midst of Judea's land in the days of the royal bard, but it is clear to readers of the Scriptures that David was the subject of spiritual throes and pangs of the most intense kind. His bosom throbbed and heaved like that of a man made fit to be the leader of a great revival. What yearnings he had—he thirsted after God, after the living God! What petitions he poured forth that God would visit Zion, and make the vine which He had planted to flourish once again. Even when his own sins pressed heavily upon him, he could not end his personal confession without entreating the Lord to build the walls of Jerusalem, and to do good in His good pleasure to Zion. Now, David was only the mouth of hundreds of others, who with equal fervency cried unto God that the blessing might rest upon His people. There was much soul travail in Israel and Judah, and the result was that the Lord was glorified, and true religion flourished.

Remember also the days of Joshua, the king. You know well how the

Book of the Law was found neglected in the temple, and when it was brought before the king, he rent his clothes, for he saw that the nation had revolted, and that wrath must come upon it to the uttermost. The young king's heart, which was tender, for he feared God, was ready to break with anguish to think of the misery that would come upon his people on account of their sins. Then there came a glorious reformation, which purged the land of idols, and caused the Passover to be observed as never before. Travail of heart among the godly produced the delightful change.

It was the same with the work of Nehemiah. His book begins with a description of the travail of his heart. He was a patriot, a man of nervous, excitable temperament, and keen sensibility for God's honor, and when his soul had felt great bitterness and longing, then he arose to build, and a blessing rested on his efforts.

In the early dawn of Christian history, there was a preparation of the church before it received an increase. Look at the obedient disciples sitting in the upper room, waiting with anxious hope; every heart there had been plowed with anguish by the death of the Lord, each one was intent to receive the promised boon of the Spirit. There, with one heart and one mind, they tarried, but not without wrestling prayer, and so the Comforter was given, and three thousand souls were given also.

The like living zeal and vehement desire have always been perceptible in the church of God before any season of refreshing. Think not that Luther was the only man that wrought the Reformation. There were hundreds who sighed and cried in secret in the cottages of the Black Forest, in the homes of Germany, and on the hills of Switzerland. There were hearts breaking for the Lord's appearing in strange places: they might have been found in the palaces of Spain, in the dungeons of the Inquisition, among the canals of Holland, and the green lanes of England. Women, as they hid their Bibles, lest their lives should be forfeited, cried out in spirit, "O God, how long?" There were pains as of a woman in travail, in secret places there were tears and bitter lamentations, on the high places of the field there were mighty strivings of sprit, and so at length there came that grand convulsion which made the Vatican to rock and reel from its foundation to its pinnacle. There has been evermore in the history of the church the travail before there has been the result.

And this, dear friends, while it is true on the large scale, is true also in every individual case. A man with no sensibility or compassion for other men's souls, may accidentally be the means of a conversion; the good word which he utters will not cease to be good because the speaker had no right to declare God's statutes. The bread and meat which were brought to Elijah were not less nourishing because the ravens brought them, but the ravens remained ravens still. A hardhearted man may say a good thing which God will bless, but, as a rule, those who bring souls to Christ are those who first of all have felt an agony of desire that souls should be saved. This is imaged to us in our Master's character. He is the great Savior of men, but before He could save others, He learned in their flesh to sympathize with them. He wept over Jerusalem, He sweat great drops of blood in Gethsemane; He was, and is, a high priest who is touched with the feeling of our infirmities. As the captain of our salvation, in bringing many sons to glory, He was made perfect by sufferings. Even Christ went not forth to preach until He had spent nights in intercessory prayer, and uttered strong cryings and tears for the salvation of His hearers. His ministering servants who have been most useful have always been eagerly desirous to be so. If any minister can be satisfied without conversions he shall have no conversions. God will not force usefulness on any man. It is only when our hearts break to see men saved that we shall be likely to see sinners' hearts broken. The secret of success lies in all-consuming zeal, all-subduing travail of souls. Read the sermons of Wesley and of Whitfield, and what is there in them? It is no severe criticism to say that they are scarcely worthy to have survived, and yet those sermons wrought marvels, and well they might, for both preachers could truly say—

> The love of Christ doth me constrain
> To seek the wandering souls of men;
> With cries, entreaties, tears, to save,
> To snatch them from the fiery wave.

In order to understand such preaching, you need to see and hear the man; you want his tearful eye, his glowing countenance, his pleading tone, his bursting heart. I have heard of a great preacher who objected to have his sermons printed, "Because," said he, "you cannot print *me*." That observation is very much to the point. A soulwinner throws himself into what he says. As I have sometimes said, we must ram ourselves into our cannons, we must fire ourselves at our hearers, and when we do this, then, by God's grace, their hearts are often carried by storm. Do any of you desire your children's conversions? You shall have them saved when you agonize for them. Many a parent who has been privileged to see his son walking in the truth will tell you that before the blessing came, he had spent many hours in prayer and in earnest pleading with God, and then it was that the Lord visited his child and renewed his soul. I have heard of a young man who had grown up and left the parental roof and through evil influences had been enticed into holding skeptical views. His father and mother were both earnest Christians, and it almost broke their hearts to see their son so opposed to the Redeemer. On one occasion they induced him to go with them to hear a celebrated minister. He accompanied them simply to please them, and for no higher motive. The sermon happened to be upon the glories of heaven. It was a very extraordinary sermon, and was calculated to make every Christian in the audience leap for joy. The young man was much gratified with the eloquence of the preacher, but nothing more; he gave him credit for superior oratorical ability, and was interested in the sermon, but felt none of its power. He chanced to look at his father and mother during the discourse, and was surprised to see them weeping. He could not imagine why they, being Christian people, should sit and weep under a sermon which was most jubilant in its strain. When he reached home, he said, "Father, we have had a capital sermon, but I could not understand what could make you sit there and cry, and my mother too?" His father said, "My dear son, I certainly had no reason to weep concerning myself, nor your mother, but I could not help thinking all through the sermon about you, for alas, I have no hope that you will be a partaker in the bright joys which await the righteous. It breaks my heart to think that you will be shut out of heaven." His mother said, "The very same thoughts crossed my mind, and the more the preacher spoke of the joys of the saved, the more I sorrowed for my dear boy that he should never know what they were." That touched the young man's heart, led him to seek his father's God, and before long he was at the same communion table, rejoicing in the God and Savior whom his parents worshiped. The travail comes before the bringing forth; the earnest anxiety, the deep emotion within, precede our being made the instruments of the salvation of others.

I think I have established the fact; now for a minute or two let me show you *the reasons for it*. Why is it that there must be this anxiety before desirable results are gained? For answer, it might suffice us to say that God has so appointed it. It is the order of nature. The child is not born into the world without the sorrows of the mother, nor is the bread which sustains life procured from the earth without toil: "In the sweat of thy face shalt thou eat bread," was a part of the primeval curse. Now, as it is in the natural, so is it in the spiritual; there shall not come the blessing we seek without first of all the earnest yearning for it. Why, it is so even in ordinary business. We say, "No sweat no sweet," "No pains no gains," "No mill no meal." If there be no labor there shall be no profit. He that would be rich must toil for it; he that would acquire fame must spend and be spent to win it. It is ever so. There must ever be the travail and then the desire comes. God has so appointed it; let us accept the decree.

But better still, He has ordained this for our good. If souls were given us without any effort, anxiety, or prayer, it would be our loss to have it so, because the anxieties which throb within a compassionate spirit exercise his graces; they produce grateful love to God; they try his faith in the power of God to save others; they drive him to the mercy seat; they strengthen his patience and perseverance; every grace within the man is educated and increased by his travail for souls. As labor is now a blessing, so also is soul-travail; men are fashioned more fully into the likeness of

Christ thereby, and the whole church is by the same motion quickened into energy. The fire of our own spiritual lives is fanned by that same breath which our prayers invite to come from the four winds to breathe upon the slain. Besides, dear friends, the zeal that God excites within us is often the means of effecting the purpose which we desire. After all God does not give conversions to eloquence, but to heart. The power in the hand of God's Spirit for conversions is heart coming into contact with heart. Truth from the heart goes to the heart. This is God's battle-ax and weapons of war in His crusade. He is pleased to use the yearnings, longings, and sympathies of Christian men as the means of compelling the careless to think, constraining the hardened to feel, and driving the unbelieving to consider. I have little confidence in elaborate speech and polished sentences as the means of reaching men's hearts, but I have real faith in that simple Christian woman who must have souls converted or she will weep her eyes out over them; and in that humble Christian who prays day and night in secret, and then avails himself of every opportunity to address a loving word to sinners. The emotion we feel, and the affection we bear, are the most powerful implements of soulwinning. God the Holy Spirit usually breaks hard hearts by tender hearts.

Besides, the travail qualifies for the proper taking care of the offspring. God does not commit His newborn children to people who do not care to see conversions. If He ever allows them to fall into such hands, they suffer very serious loss thereby. Who is so fit to encourage a newborn believer as the man who first anguished before the Lord for his conversion? Those you have wept over and prayed for you will be sure to encourage and assist. The church that never travailed, should God send her a hundred converts, would be unfit to train them; she would not know what to do with little children, and would leave them to much suffering. Let us thank God, brethren, if He has given us any degree of the earnest anxiety and sympathy which mark soulwinning men and women, and let us ask to have more; for, in proportion as we have it, we shall be qualified to be the instruments in the hand of the Spirit, nursing and cherishing God's sons and daughters.

Once more, there is a great benefit in the law which makes travail necessary to spiritual birth, because it secures all the glory to God. If you want to be lowered in your own esteem, try to convert a child. I would like those brethren who believe so much in free will, and the natural goodness of the human heart, to try some children that I could bring to them, and see whether they could break their hearts and make them love the Savior. Why, sir, you never think yourself so great a fool as after trying in your own strength to bring a sinner to the Savior. Oh! how often have I come back defeated from arguing with an awakened person whom I have sought to comfort; I did think I had some measure of skill in handling sorrowful cases, but I have been compelled to say to myself, "What a simpleton I am!

God the Holy Spirit must take this case in hand, for I am foiled." When one has tried in a sermon to reach a certain person who is living in sin, one learns afterward that he enjoyed the sermon which he ought to have smarted under; then, you say, "Ah, now I see what a weak worm I am, and if good be done God shall have the glory." Your longing then that others should be saved, and your vehemence of spirit, shall secure to God all the glory of His own work; this is what the Lord is aiming at, for His glory He will not give to another, nor His praise to an arm of flesh.

And now, having established the fact, and shown the reasons for it, let us notice *how this travail shows itself.*

Usually when God intends greatly to bless a church, it will begin in this way: Two or three persons in it are distressed at the low state of affairs, and become troubled even to anguish. Perhaps they do not speak to one another, or know of their common grief, but they begin to pray with flaming desire and untiring importunity. The passion to see the church revived rules them. They think of it when they go to rest, they dream of it on their beds, they muse on it in the streets. This one thing eats them up. They suffer great heaviness and continual sorrow in heart for perishing sinners; they travail in birth for souls. I have happened to become the center of certain brethren in this church; one of them said to me the other day, "O sir, I pray day and night for God to prosper our church: I long to see greater things, God is blessing us, but we want much more." I saw the deep earnestness of the man's soul, and I thanked him and thanked God heartily, thinking it to be a sure sign of a coming blessing. Sometime after, another friend, who probably now hears me speak, but who did not know anything about the other, felt the same yearning, and must needs let me know it; he too is anxious, longing, begging, crying, for a revival. Thus from three or four quarters I have had the same message, and I feel hopeful because of these tokens for good. When the sun rises the mountain tops first catch the light, and those who constantly live near to God will be the first to feel the influence of the coming refreshing. The Lord give me a dozen importunate pleaders and lovers of souls, and by His grace we will shake all London from end to end yet. The work would go on without the mass of you, Christians; many of you only hinder the march of the army, but give us a dozen lionlike, lamblike men burning with intense love to Christ and souls, and nothing will be impossible to their faith. The most of us are not worthy to unloose the shoelaces of ardent saints. I often feel I am not so myself, but I aspire and long to be reckoned among them. Oh, may God give us this first sign of the travail in the earnest ones and twos.

By degrees the individuals are drawn together by sacred affinity, and the prayer meetings become very different. The brother who talked twenty minutes of what he called prayer, and yet never asked for a single thing, gives up his oration and falls to pleading with many tears and broken sentences, while the friend who used to relate his experience and go through the doctrines of grace, and call that a prayer, forgets that rigmarole and begins agonizing before the throne. And not only this, but little knots here and there come together in their cottages, and in their little rooms cry mightily to God. The result will be that the minister, even if he does not know of the feeling in the hearts of his people, will grow fervent himself. He will preach more evangelically, more tenderly, more earnestly. He will be no longer formal, or cold, or stereotyped; he will be all alive. Meanwhile, not with the preacher only will be the blessing, but with his hearers who love the Lord. One will be trying a plan for getting in the young people; another will be looking after the strangers in the aisles, who come only now and then. One brother will make a vehement attempt to preach the Gospel at the corner of the street; another will open a room down a dark court; another will visit lodging houses and hospitals. All sorts of holy plans will be invented, and zeal will break out in many directions. All this will be spontaneous, nothing will be forced. If you want to get up a revival, as the term is, you can do it, just as you can grow tasteless strawberries in winter by artificial heat. There are ways and means of doing that kind of thing, but the genuine work of God needs no such planning and scheming; it is altogether spontaneous. If you see a snowdrop next February in your garden, you will feel persuaded that spring is on the way; the artificial flower-maker could put as many snowdrops there as you please, but that would be no index of coming spring. So you may get up an apparent zeal which will be no proof of God's blessing; but when fervor comes of itself, without human direction or control, then is it of the Lord. When men's hearts heave and break, like the mold of the garden under the influence of the reviving life which lay buried there, then in very deed a benediction is on the way. Travail is no mockery, but a real agony of the whole nature. May such be seen in this our church, and throughout the whole Israel of God.

Travail Is Frequently Followed by Surprising Results

Now, with great brevity, let us consider that the result is often very surprising. It is frequently surprising for *rapidity*. "As soon as Zion travailed, she brought forth her children." God's works are not tied by time. The more spiritual a force is the less it lies within the chains of time. The electric current, which has a greater nearness to the spiritual than the grosser forms of materialism, is inconceivably rapid from that very reason, and by it time is all but annihilated. The influences of the Spirit of God are a force most spiritual, and more quick than anything beneath the sun. As soon as we agonize in soul the Holy Spirit can, if He pleases, convert the person for whom we have pleaded. While we are yet speaking He hears, and before we call He answers. Some calculate the expected progress of a church by arithmetic, and I think I have heard of arithmetical sermons in which there have been ingenious calculations as to how many missionaries it would take to convert the world, and how much cash would be demanded. Now there is no room here for the application of mathematics; spiritual forces are not calculable by an arithmetic which is most at home in the material universe. A truth which is calculated to strike the mind of one man today may readily enough produce a like effect upon a million minds tomorrow. The preaching which moves one heart needs not to be altered to tell upon ten thousand. With God's Spirit our present instrumentalities will suffice to win the world to Jesus; without Him, ten thousand times as much apparent force would be only so much weakness. The spread of truth, moreover, is not reckonable by time. During the ten years which ended in 1870, such wondrous changes were wrought throughout the world that no prophet would have been believed had he foretold them. Reforms have been accomplished in England, in the United States, in Germany, in Spain, in Italy, which, according to ordinary reckoning, would have occupied at least one hundred years. Things which concern the mind cannot be subjected to those regulations of time which govern steamboats and railways; in such matters God's messengers are flames of fire. The Spirit of God is able to operate upon the minds of men instantaneously: witness the case of Paul. Between now and tomorrow morning He could excite holy thought in all the minds of all the thousand millions of the sons of Adam; and if prayer were mighty enough, and strong enough, why should it not be done on some bright day? We are not restricted in Him, we are restricted in our own hearts. All the fault lies there. Oh, for the travail that would produce immediate results.

But the result is surprising, not only for its rapidity, but for *the greatness of it.* It is said, "Shall a nation be born at once?" for as soon as ever Zion was in distress about her children, tens of thousands came and built up Jerusalem, and reestablished the fallen state. So in answer to prayer, God does not only give speedy blessings, but great blessings. There were fervent prayers in that upper room "before the day of Pentecost had fully come," and what a great answer it was when, after Peter's sermon, some three thousand were ready to confess their faith in Christ, and to be baptized. Shall we never see such things again? Is the Spirit limited? Has His arm waxed short? Nay, verily, but we clog and hinder Him. He cannot do any mighty work here because of our unbelief; if our unbelief were cast out, and if prayer went up to God with eagerness, and vehemence, and importunity, then would a blessing descend so copious as to amaze us all.

But enough of this, for I must needs pass on to the next point.

This Travail and Its Result Are Abundantly Desirable

The world is perishing for lack of knowledge. Did any one among us ever lay China on his heart? Your imagination cannot grapple with the population of that mighty empire without God, without Christ, strangers to the commonwealth of Israel. But it is not China alone; there are other vast nations lying in darkness; the great serpent has coiled himself around the globe, and who shall set the world free from him? Reflect upon this one city with its three millions. What sin the moon sees! What sin the Sabbath sees! Alas! for the transgressions of this wicked city. Babylon of old could not have been worse than London is, nor so guilty, for she had not the light that London has received. Brethren, there is no hope for China, no hope for the world, no hope for our own city, while the church is sluggish and lethargic. It is through the church the blessing is bestowed. Christ multiplies the bread, and gives it to the disciples; the multitudes can only get it through the disciples. Oh, it is time, it is high time that the churches were awakened to seek the good of dying myriads. Moreover, brethren, the powers of evil are ever active. We may sleep, but Satan sleeps never. The church's plow lies yonder, rusting in the furrow; do you not see it, to your shame? But the plow of Satan goes from end to end of his great field, he leaves no headland, but he plows deep while sluggish churches sleep. May we be stirred as we see the awful activity of evil spirits and persons who are under their sway. How industriously pernicious literature is spread abroad, and with what a zeal do men seek for fresh ways of sinning. He is eminent among men who can invent fresh songs to gratify the lascivious tongue, or find new spectacles to delight unclean eyes. O God, are Your enemies awake, and only Your friends asleep? O Sufferer, once bathed in bloody sweat in Gethsemane, is there not one of the Twelve awake but Judas? Are they all asleep except the traitor? May God arouse us for His infinite mercy's sake.

Besides this, my brethren, when a church is not serving God, mischief is brewing within herself. While she is not bringing others in, her own heart is becoming weak in its pulsations, and her entire constitution is a prey to decline. The church must either bring forth children to God, or die of consumption; she has no alternative but that. A church must either be fruitful or rot, and of all things a rotting church is the most offensive. Would God we could bury our dead churches out of our sight, as Abraham buried Sarah, for above ground they breed a pestilence of skepticism, for men say, "Is this religion?" and taking it to be so, they forego true religion altogether.

And then, worst of all is, God is not glorified. If there be no yearning of heart in the church, and no conversions, where is the travail of the Redeemer's soul? Where, Immanuel, where are the trophies of Your terrible conflict? Where are the jewels for Your crown? You shall have Your own, Your Father's will shall not be frustrated; You shall be adored, but as yet we see it not. Hard are men's hearts, and they will not love You; unyielding are their wills, and they will not own Your sovereignty. Oh! weep because Jesus is not honored. The foul oath still curdles our blood as we hear it, and blasphemy usurps the place of grateful song. Oh! by the wounds and bloody sweat, by the cross, and nails, and spear, I beseech you, followers of Christ, be in earnest, that Jesus Christ's name may be known and loved through the earnest agonizing endeavors of the Christian church.

Woe to Those Who Hinder the Travail of the Church

And now I must come near to a close, by, in the fourth place, noticing the woe which will surely come to those who hinder the travail of the church, and so prevent the bringing forth of her children. An earnest spirit cannot complete its exhortations to zeal without pronouncing a denunciation upon the indifferent. What said the heroine of old who had gone forth against the enemies of Israel, when she remembered coward spirits? "Curse ye, Meroz, saith the angel of the Lord, curse ye bitterly the inhabitants thereof; because they came not to the help of the Lord, against the mighty." Some such curse will assuredly come upon every professing Christian who is backward in helping the church in the day of her soul's travail. And who are they that hinder her? I answer, every worldly Christian hinders the progress of the Gospel. Every member of a church who is living in secret sin, who is tolerating in his heart anything that he knows to be wrong, who is not seeking eagerly his own personal sancti- fication, is to that extent hindering the work of the Spirit of God. Be clean you who bear the vessels of the Lord, for to the extent that you maintain known unholiness, you restrain the Spirit. He cannot work by us as long as any conscious sin is tolerated. It is not overt breaking of commandments that I am now speaking of, brethren, but I include worldliness also—a care for carnal things, and a carelessness about spiritual things, having enough grace just to make us hope that you are a Christian, but not enough to prove you are; bearing a shriveled apple here and there on the topmost bough but not much fruit—this I mean, this partial barrenness, not com- plete enough to condemn, yet complete enough to restrain the blessing, this robs the treasury of the church, and hinders her progress. O brethren, if any of you are thus described, repent and do your first works; and God help you to be foremost in proportion as you have been behind.

They are also guilty who distract the mind of the church from the sub- ject in hand. Anybody who calls off the thoughts of the church from soul-saving is a mischief maker. I have heard it said of a minister, "He greatly influences the politics of the town." Well, it is a very doubtful good in my mind, a very doubtful good indeed. If the man, keeping to his own calling of preaching the Gospel happens to influence these meaner things, it is well, but any Christian minister, who thinks that he can do two things well, is mistaken. Let him mind soulwinning, and not turn a Christian church into a political club. Let us fight out our politics somewhere else, but not inside the church of God. There our one business is soulwinning, our one banner is the cross, our one leader is the crucified King. Inside the church there may be minor things that take off the thoughts of men from seeking souls—little things that can be made beneath the eye that is microscopical to swell into great offenses. O my brethren, let us while souls are perishing waive personal difference. "It must need be that offenses come, but woe unto him by whom the offense cometh"; but after all what can there be that is worth taking notice of, compared with glorifying Christ. If our Lord and Master would be honored by your being a doormat for His saints to wipe their feet on, you would be honored to be in the position; and if there shall come glory to God by your patient endurance, even of insult and contumely, be glad in your heart that you are permitted to be nothing, that Christ may be all in all. We must by no means turn aside to this or that; not even golden apples must tempt us in this race! There lies the mark, and until it is reached, we must never pause, but onward press, for Christ's cause and crown.

Above all, my brethren, we shall be hindering the travail of the church if we do not share in it. Many church members think that if they do nothing wrong, and make no trouble, then they are all right. Not at all, sir; not at all. Here is a chariot, and we are all engaged to drag it. Some of you do not put out your hands to pull; well, then, the rest of us have to labor so much the more, and the worst of it is we have to draw you also. While you do not add to the strength which draws, you increase the weight that is to be drawn. It is all very well for you to say, "But I do not hinder"; you do hinder, you cannot help hindering. If a man's leg does not help him in walking, it certainly hinders him. Oh, I cannot bear to think of it. That I should be a hindrance to my own soul's growth is bad indeed, but that I should stand in the way of the people of God and cool their courage, and damp their ardor—my Master, let it never be! Sooner let me sleep among the clods of the valley than be a hindrance to the meanest work that is done for Your name.

A Word of Blessing

And now I shall close, not with this note of woe, but with a word of blessing. Depend upon it there shall come a great blessing to any of you who feel the soul travail that brings souls to God. You own heart will be watered. You know the old illustration, so often used that it is now almost hackneyed, of the two travelers who passed a man frozen in the snow, and thought to be dead; and the one said, "I have enough to do to keep myself alive, I will hasten on"; but the other said, "I cannot pass a fellow creature while there is the least breath in him." He stooped down and began to warm the frozen man by rubbing him with great vigor, and at last the poor fellow opened his eyes, came back to life and animation, and walked along with the man who had restored him to life; and what think you was one of the first sights they saw? It was the man who must needs take care of himself—frozen to death. The good Samaritan had preserved his own life by rubbing the other man; the friction he had given had caused the action of his own blood, and kept him in vigor. You will bless yourselves if you bless others.

Moreover, will it not be a joy to feel that you have done what you could? It is always well on a Sunday evening for a preacher to feel when he gets home, "Well, I may not have preached as I would wish, but I have preached the Lord Jesus and preached all my heart out, and I could do no more." He sleeps soundly on that. After a day spent in doing all the good you can, even if you have met with no success, you can lean your head on Christ's bosom and fall asleep, feeling that if souls be not gathered, yet you have your reward. If men are lost, it is some satisfaction to us that they were not lost because we failed to tell them the way of salvation. But what a comfort it will be to you supposing you should be successful in bringing some to Christ. Why it will make all the bells of your soul to ring. There is no greater joy, except the joy of our own communion with Christ, than this of bringing others to trust the Savior. Oh, seek this joy and pant after it. And what if you should see your own children converted? You have long hoped for it, but your hopes have been disappointed; God means to give you that choice blessing when you live more nearly to Him yourself. Yes, wife, the husband's heart will be won when your heart is perfectly consecrated. Yes, mother, the girl shall love the Savior when you love Him better. Yes, teacher, God means to bless your class, but not until first of all He has made you fit to receive the blessing. Why, now, if your children were to be converted through your teaching, you would be mightily proud of it; God knows you could not bear such success, and does not mean to give it until He has laid you low at His feet, and emptied you of yourself, and filled you with Himself.

And now I ask the prayers of all this church, that God would send us a time of revival. I do not complain that I have labored in vain, and spent my strength for nought; far from it. I have not even a thought that the blessing is withdrawn from the preaching of the Word, even in a measure, for I never had so many cases of conversion in my life as I have known since I have been restored from sickness; I have never before received so many letters in so short a time, telling me that the sermons printed have been blest, or the sermons preached here; yet I do not think we ever had so few conversions from the regular congregation. I partly account for it from the fact that you cannot fish in one pond always and catch as many fish as at first. Perhaps the Lord has saved all of you He means to save; sometimes, I am afraid He has; and then it will be little use my keeping on preaching to you, and I had better shift quarters and try somewhere else. It would be a melancholy thought if I believed it—I do not believe it, I only fear it. Surely it is not always to be true that strangers, who drop in here only once are converted, and you who are always hearing the Gospel remain unaffected. Strange, but may it not be strangely, lamentably true of you? This very day may the anxiety of your Christian friends be excited for you, and then may you be led to be anxious for yourselves, and give your eyes no slumber until you find the Savior. You know the way of salvation; it is simply to come with your sins and rest them on the Savior; it is to rely upon or trust in the atoning blood. Oh, that you may be made to trust this morning, to the praise of the glory of His grace. The elders mean to meet together tomorrow evening to have a special hour of prayer; I hope, also, the mothers will meet and have a time of wrestling in prayer, and that every member of the church will try to set apart a time for supplication this week, that the Lord may visit again His church, and cause us to rejoice in His name. We cannot go back; we dare not go back. We have put hand to plow, and the curse will be upon us if we turn back. Remember Lot's wife. It must be onward with us; backward it cannot be. In the name of God the Eternal, let us gird ourselves by the power of His Spirit, and go onward conquering through the blood of the Lamb. We ask it for Jesus' sake. Amen.

13

Conversions Encouraged

But if from thence thou shalt seek the Lord thy God, thou shalt find him, if thou seek him with all thy heart and with all thy soul. When thou art in tribulation, and all these things are come upon thee, even in the latter days, if thou turn to the Lord thy God, and shalt be obedient unto his voice; (for the Lord thy God is a merciful God;) he will not forsake thee, neither destroy thee, nor forget the covenant of thy fathers which he sware unto them (Deuteronomy 4:29–31).

L ast Sunday the title of my discourse was "Conversions Desired," and my earnest prayer to God has been that the effect of this morning's sermon may be conversions accomplished. I cannot be happy unless I indulge the hope that some will this morning turn to God with full purpose of heart, led to do so by the power of divine grace. For this I sought the Lord, and at this I resolved to aim. I asked myself, "What is the most likely subject in the hand of the Holy Spirit to lead to the Lord? Shall I preach the terrors of the Lord, or shall I proclaim the sweetness of divine mercy? Each of these has its proper use, but which will be most likely to answer our design today?" I remembered the fable of the sun and the wind. These rival powers competed as to which could compel the traveler to cast away his cloak. The wind blew boisterously, and tugged at the garment as if it would tear it from the traveler's shoulders, but he buttoned it the closer about him and held it firmly with his hand. The battle was not to the strong and threatening. Then the sun burst forth from behind a cloud, when the wind had ceased its blustering, and smiled upon the traveler with warmth of kindness until he loosened his cloak, and by and by was glad to take it off altogether: the soft, sweet influence of the sun had vanquished where the storm had raged in vain. So I thought, perhaps if I preach the tender mercy of God, and His readiness to forgive, it may be to my hearers as

This sermon was taken from *The Metropolitan Tabernacle Pulpit* and was preached on Sunday morning, March 12, 1876.

the warm beams of the sun to the traveler, and they will cast away the garments of their sin and self-righteousness. I know that the arrows of love are keen, and wound many hearts which are invulnerable to the sword of wrath. O that these sacred darts win the victory this day! When ships at sea apprehend a storm they will gladly make for an open harbor, but if it be doubtful whether they can enter the port they will rather weather the tempest than run the risk of being unable to enter the harbor's mouth. Some havens can only be entered when the tide happens to be at the flood, and therefore the captain will not venture; but when the welcome signals are flying and it is clear that there is plenty of water, and that they may safely run behind the breakwater, they hesitate no longer, but make sail for the shelter. Let seeking souls know this day that the Lord's harbor of refuge is open, the port of free grace can be reached, that there is sea room for the hugest transgressor, and love enough to float the greatest sinner into port. Ho, weather-beaten vessels, you may come and welcome! There is no need that even for a solitary hour you should run the risk of the tempest of almighty wrath; you are invited to find shelter and to enjoy it now.

It is rather singular that having these ideas floating in my mind, and desiring to preach free grace and abounding mercy, I would have found my text in Deuteronomy. Why, that is a book of the law, and is plentifully besprinkled with terrible threatenings, and yet I find a Gospel theme in it, yea, and one if the very richest! As I read it I admired it for its connection as well as for its own fullness, it seems to me so pleasant to find this lily among thorns. As in the wintry months of the opening year one finds a crocus smiling up from the cold soil and in its golden cup offering a taste of the sunlight which summer will more fully bring, so amid the ungenial pages of the law I see this precious Gospel declaration, which like the spring flower assures us that God's love is yet alive, and will bring us happier times. My thoughts also likened this passage to the water which leaped from the smitten rock, for the law is like a rock, and the Pentateuch is hard and stern as granite; but here in its very bowels we find a crystal spring of which the thirsty may drink. I likened the text also to the manna lying on the desert sand, the bread of heaven glittering like a shining pearl upon the barren soil of the wilderness. Here amid the fiery statutes of the law, and the terrible judgments threatened by the God of Sinai you see this manna of mercy dropped about your tents this morning, as fresh, I hope to you as if but newly fallen. May you eat of it and live forever.

Let us come to our text at once. The Lord here encourages sinners to turn to Himself, and find abundant grace. He encourages sinners who had violated His plainest commandments, who had made idols, and so had corrupted themselves, and had consequently been visited with captivity, and other chastisements—He invites them to turn from their evil ways and seek His face. I feel moved to say at the commencement this discourse that if the text has any limited aspect, if it is to be regarded as uttered to any special character among transgressors, it peculiarly belongs to *backsliders*, for the people to whom it was first addressed were the people of God, but they had set up idols, and so had wandered; it is to them chiefly, though not to them exclusively, that these encouragements to repentance are presented. As probably there are some backsliders here who once stood in the church of God, but have been cut off therefrom, who once were very zealous and earnest in the cause of God, but have now become utterly indifferent to all religion, I charge such to take this text home to themselves. Take every syllable of it into your own heart, backslider. Read, mark, learn, and inwardly digest the same, and may the text bring you to your knees and to your God. It gives you a pointed invitation to return from your wanderings and end your weary backslidings by coming once more to your Father's house, for He will not forsake you, nor destroy you, nor forget the covenant of mercy which He has made on your behalf. Happy are you that you may return; happy shall I be if you do return. I thought I would lay special stress upon this, because the Lord Himself, and His ministers with Him, rejoice more over one lost sheep that returns to the Shepherd of souls than over ninety and nine that went not astray. There is rejoicing when a man finds a treasure which he never had before, but it is scarcely equal to the joy of the woman who found the piece of money which was hers already, but which she had lost. Glad is the house when the babe is born, but deeper is the joy when the lost son is found. My soul longs to see the Lord bring home His banished ones, and to be the means of gathering His scattered ones.

Still, the text is fully applicable to all sinners—to all who have corrupted themselves and done evil in the sight of the Lord to provoke Him to anger. The Ever-merciful encourages them to turn to Him with full purpose of heart, by assuring them that He will not forsake them. There seems to me to be in the text three points which should induce an earnest seeking of His face at once, for here is, first, *a time mentioned*; secondly, *a way appointed*; thirdly, *encouragement given*.

A Time Mentioned

First, then, in the text there is a time mentioned. Look at it: "If from thence thou shalt seek the Lord. . . . When thou art in tribulation, and all these things are come upon thee, even in the latter days."

The time in which the Lord bids you seek Him, O you unforgiven ones, is first of all, "*from thence*," that is, from the condition into which you have fallen, or the position which you now occupy. According to the connection of the text, the offending Israelites were supposed to be in captivity, scattered among various nations, dwelling where they were compelled to worship gods of wood and stone which could not see, nor hear, nor feel, nor eat, nor smell; yet "from thence"—from the unhallowed heathen villages, from their lone sorrows by the waters of Babylon, from their captivity in far-off Chaldea, they were bidden to turn to the Lord and obey His voice. Their surroundings were not to be allowed to hinder their prayers. Perhaps, dear friend, at this time you are dwelling among ungodly relations; if you begin to speak about religion you are put down at once, you hear nothing that can help you in the way to better things, but very much that would hinder you; nevertheless, do not delay, but "from thence," even from there seek you the Lord, for it is written: "If thou seek him he will be found of thee." It may be you are living in a neighborhood where everything is hostile to the Gospel of Jesus Christ, and injurious even to your morals. Time was, and you may remember it with regret, when you were a child upon the knee of a pious mother, when you spent your Sundays in the Sunday school, when the Bible was read in your house every day; but now all these helps are taken from you, and everything around is dragging you down to greater and yet greater sin. Do not, however, make this a reason for delay; as well might a man refuse to go to a physician because he lives in an unhealthy locality, or a drowning man refuse the lifeboat because a raging sea surrounds him. Hasten rather than slacken your speed. Do not tarry until your position improve; do not wait until you move into a godly family, or live nearer to the means of grace, for if you seek Him "from thence" He will be found of you.

But you will tell me that it is not so much your regret that others are ungodly among whom you dwell, but that you yourself are in a wretched condition of heart, for you have followed after one sin and another until evil has become a habit with you, and you cannot shake it off. Like a rolling thing before the whirlwind you are driven on; an awful force impels you from bad to worse. Arouse yourself, O man, for immediate action, for if you delay to turn to God until you are free from the dominion of sin, then assuredly you will wait forever, and perish in your folly. If you could vanquish evil by your own power you would not need to seek the Lord, for you would have found salvation in yourself; be not so infatuated as to dream of such a thing. Today, "from thence," from the place where you now are, turn your face to your Father who is in heaven, and seek Him through Jesus Christ. Recollect the hymn which ought to be sung every Sunday in our assemblies—

> Just as I am—and waiting not
> To rid my soul of one dark blot,
> To thee, whose blood can cleanse each spot,
>   O Lamb of God, I come.

Every verse begins with "Just as I am," and so must your prayer, your faith, your hope begin. The whole hymn commences "Just as I am," and so must your Christian life be started.

The Lord invites you as you are and where you are. Are you one of a godless family, the only one in the house who has felt any serious thought at all? Come, then, and tarry not, for the Lord invited you. Are you the one man in a large workshop where all the rest are irreligious? Admire His sovereign grace, accept the call, and henceforth be the Lord's. The Lord invites those of you who have gone to the ends of the earth in sin, and have brought yourselves into captivity by your rebellion. Today, even today, He bids you seek Him "with all your heart and with all your soul."

With regard to the time of turning, it is well worthy of our notice that we are specially encouraged to turn to the Lord if we are in a painful plight. Our text says, *"When thou art in tribulation."* Are you sick? Have you felt ill for some time? Does your weakness increase upon you? Are you apprehensive that this sickness may even be to death? When you are in such tribulation then you may return to Him. A sick body should lead us the more earnestly to seek healing for a sick soul. Are you poor, have you come down from a comfortable position to one of hard labor and of scant provision? When you are in this tribulation then turn to the Lord, for He has sent you this need to make you see your yet greater necessity, even your need of Him. The empty purse should make you remember your soul poverty, the bare cupboard should lead you to see the emptiness of all your carnal confidences, and accumulating debts should compel you to calculate how much you owe to your Lord. It is possible that your trials are very bitter at this moment, because you are expecting to lose some whom you dearly love, and this is like rending half yourself away. One dear child is hardly cold in the tomb, and your heart is bleeding when you think of this loss—and now another is sickening and will follow the first. When you are in this tribulation, then be sure to seek the Lord; for His pitying heart is open to you, and He will sanctify this grief to noblest purposes. Is it possible that I speak to one whose sins have become so open as to have been punished by the law of the land? Have you lost your character? Will none employ you any longer? When you are in this tribulation then turn to your Lord, for He will receive earth's castaways, and make criminals His sons. Have you suffered from the just verdict of society because you are vicious, dishonest, and disreputable? Are you at this time despised and looked down upon? Yet even to you would I say, when you are in tribulation, when every door is shut, when all hands are held up against you, even then seek the Lord, and He will be found of you. If your father scarcely dares to think upon your name, if you have been a grief to your sister's heart, and have brought your mother's gray hairs with sorrow to the grave, yet now, even in this shameful estate, when you are in tribulation turn to the Lord your God.

Doubtless there are some people who will never be saved except they come into tribulation. Their substance must all be spent, and a mighty

famine must come upon them, the citizens of the far country must refuse
them aid, and with hungry bellies they must stand at the trough and be willing to feed with the swine, or else it will never occur to them to say, "I will
arise and go to my father." No matter how deep your trouble, your safest
and wisest course is to flee to God in Christ Jesus, and put your trust in
Him.

Notice further, when you feel that the judgments of God have begun to
overtake you, then you may come to Him: "When thou art in tribulation
and *all these things* [these threatened things] *are come upon thee.*" There
are many in this world who feel as if their sin had at last found them out,
and had commenced to be a hell to them. The manslayer has overtaken
them, and is striking at them with terrible blows. "Ah," says one, "my great
sins have provoked at last God, and all men may see what He has done to
me for He has removed my choicest mercies from me. I despised a father's
instruction—that father is dead; I did not value my mother's tears—my
mother sleeps under the sod. The dear wife who used to beg me to walk to
the house of God with her, I slighted and treated her with unkindness, and
death has removed her from my bosom. The little child that used to climb
my knee and sing its little hymns, and persuade me to pray, has gone too!
God has found me out at last, and begun to strip me. These are only the
first drops of an awful shower of wrath from which I cannot escape. Alas,
while one mercy after another is removed, my former joys have been
embittered, and are joys no more. I go to the theater as I used to do, but I
do not enjoy it. I see beneath the paint and the gilt, and it seems a mockery of my woe. My old companions come to see me, and they would sing
me the old songs, but I cannot bear them; their mirth grates on my ear—
at times it seems to be mere idiotic yelling. I used to get alone and
philosophize and dote upon many things which afforded me comfort, but
now I find no consolation in them—I have no joy of my thoughts now. The
world is dreary, and my soul is weary. I am in the sere and yellow leaf, and
all the world is fading with me. What little joy I had before has utterly
departed, and no new joy comes. I am neither fit for God nor fit for the
devil. I can find no peace in sin, and no rest in religion. Into the narrow
way I fear I cannot enter, and in the broad way I am so jostled that I do not
know how to pursue my course. Worst of all there is before me a dreadful
outlook; I am filled with horrible apprehensions of the dread hereafter. I
am afraid of the harvest which must follow the sad seed sowing of my mis-
spent life. I have a dread of death upon me; I know not how near it may be,
but it is too near, I know, and I am not prepared for it. I am overwhelmed
with thoughts of the judgment to come. I hear the trump ringing in my ears
when I am at my work. I hear the messengers of God's justice summon-
ing me and saying, 'Come to judgment, come to judgment, come away.'
A fearful sound is in mine ears, and I, whither shall I go?" Hear, O man,

and be comforted, for now is the appointed time for you to seek the Lord, for our text says, "When all these things are come upon thee, if thou turn unto the Lord thy God, he will not forsake thee neither destroy thee."

There is yet one more word which appears to me to contain great comfort in it, and it is this, *"even in the latter days."* This expression may refer to the latter days of Jewish history, though I can scarcely think it does, because the Jews are not now guilty of idolatry. I rather think it must refer to the latter days of any one of their captivities and in our case to the latter days of life. Looking around me I see that many of you are advanced in years, and if you are unconverted I thank God I am as free to preach Christ to you as if you had been children or young men. If you have spent sixty or seventy years in rebellion against your God, you may return "even in the latter days." If your day is almost over, and you have arrived at the eleventh hour, when the sun touches the horizon, and evening shadows thicken, still He may call you into His vineyard and at the close of the day give you your penny. He is longsuffering and full of mercy, not willing that any should perish, and therefore He sends me out as His messenger, to assure you that if you seek Him He will be found of you, "even in the latter days." It is a beautiful sight, though it is mingled with much sadness, to see a very old man become a babe in Christ. It is sweet to see him, after he has been so many years the proud, wayward, self-confident master of himself, at last learning wisdom, and sitting at Jesus' feet. They hang up in the cathedrals and public halls old banners which have long been carried by the enemy into the thick of the fight. If they have been torn by shot and shell, so much the more do the captors value them: the older the standard the more honor is it, it seems, to seize it as a trophy. Men boast when they have carried off—

> The flag that braved a thousand years
> The battle and the breeze.

Oh, how I wish that my Lord and Master would lay hold on some of you worn-out sinners, you have been set up by the devil as standards of sin. O that the Prince of the kings of the earth would compel you to say, "Love conquers even me."

I will not leave this head until I have said that it gives me great joy to be allowed to preach an immediate Gospel to you—a Gospel which bids you turn to God and find present salvation. Suppose for a moment that the Gospel ran thus—"You, sinner, shall be saved in twelve months time if you turn to God." Oh, sirs, I would count the days for you until the twelve months were gone. If it were written, "I will be found of you in March 1877," I would weary over you until the auspicious season arrived, and say, "Maybe they will die before mercy's hour has struck; spare them, good Lord." Yes, and if it were true that God would not hear you until next

Sunday, I should like to lock you up and keep you out of harm's way, if I could, until that time arrives, lest you should die before the promised hour. If there were any way of insuring your lives, though you had to give all that you have for your soul, you might be glad to insure your life until next Sunday. But, blessed be God, the promise does not tarry; it is NOW! "Today if you will hear His voice." The Gospel does not even bid you wait until you reach your home, or get to your bedside, but here and now, in that pew and at this moment, if you seek Him with all your heart, and with all your soul, the Lord Jesus will be found of you, and present salvation shall be immediately enjoyed. Is it not encouraging to think that *just now* the Lord is waiting to be gracious?

The Way Appointed

But now, secondly, let us look at the way appointed. To find mercy, what are we bidden to do? "If from thence thou shalt seek the Lord thy God." We have not, then, to bring anything to God, but to seek *Him*. We have not to seek a righteousness to bring to Him, nor seek a state of heart which will fit us for Him, but to seek *Him* at once. Sinner, you have offended God, none but God can forgive you, for the offenses are against Himself. Seek Him, then, that He may forgive you. It is essential that you seek Him as a real existence, and a true person, believing that He is, and that He is a rewarder of them that diligently seek Him. It is all in vain to seek sacraments, you must seek *Him*; it is idle to go through forms of prayer, or to utter customary phrases of devotion, you must seek *Him*. Your salvation lies in God, sinner, and your seeking must be after God. Do you understand this? It is not going to your priest or to your clergyman, or to your Bible or to your prayer book, or even to your knees in formal prayer; but you must draw near to God in Christ Jesus, and He must be found of you as a man finds a treasure and takes it to be his own. "But where shall I find Him?" says one. When they sought God of old they went to the mercy seat; Jesus Christ is that mercy seat, sprinkled with precious blood, and if you want to find God, you must seek Him in the person of Jesus Christ. Is it not written: "No man cometh unto the Father but by me"? Jesus is the one Mediator between God and man, and if you would find God, you must find Him in the person of Jesus the Nazarene, who is also the Son of the Highest. You will find Jesus by believing Him, trusting Him, resting upon Him. When you have trusted Jesus, you have found God in Jesus, for He has said, "He that has seen me, has seen the Father." Then have you come to God when you have believed in Jesus Christ. How simple this is! How unencumbered with subtleties and difficulties! When God gives grace, how easy and how plain is believing. We are not to be content with self, but to seek the Lord. Being nothing in ourselves, we are to go out of ourselves to Him. Being ourselves unworthy, we are to find worthiness in Jesus.

We are also to grasp the Lord as ours, for the text says. "Thou shalt seek the Lord *thy God*." Sinners, that is a part of saving faith, to take God to be *your* God; if He is only another man's God, He cannot save you; He must be yours, yours, assuredly yours, yours to trust and love and serve all your days, or you will be lost.

Now, mark God's directions: "If you seek him *with all thy heart and with all thy soul*." There must be no pretense about this seeking. If you desire to be saved, there must be no playing and toying, trifling and feigning. The search must be real, sincere, and earnest, fervent, intense, thorough-going, or it will be failure. Is this too much to ask? Surely if anything in the world deserves earnestness it is this. If anything ought to arouse all a man's powers to energy, it is the salvation of his soul. You cannot win gold and attain riches without being in earnest in the pursuit, but what earnestness does this deserve? This obtaining eternal life, deliverance from eternal death, acceptance in the Beloved, endless bliss? Oh, men, if you sleep over anything, at any rate be awake here! If you trifle upon any matters of importance, yet here at any rate be serious, solemn, and earnest. Here there must be no idling and no delay. Note that there is a repetition in the text. "If thou seek him *with all thy heart* and *with all thy soul*," we must be doubly in earnest, heart and soul must be in the pursuit. Halfhearted seeking is no seeking at all. To ask for mercy from God and at the same time to be willing to be without it is a mere pretense of asking. If you are content to be put off with an inferior blessing, you are not seeking the Lord at all. I remember one who is now a member of this church who in a desperate fit of soul anxiety said solemnly to one of us, "I will never go to work again, I will neither eat nor drink until I have found the Savior," and with that solemn resolve it was not long before he had found Him. Oh, sirs, suppose you would be lost. Suppose you would perish while I am speaking! I know of no reason why your pulse should continue to beat, or your breath should remain in your nostrils, and if at this moment you were to die, at that selfsame instant you would plunge amid the flames of hell. Escape, then, at once. Even now make soul matters your sole concern. Whatever else you have to attend to, leave it alone, and attend first to this chief thing, the salvation of your soul. If a man were in a sinking vessel, he may have been a student of the classics, but he will not think of stopping to translate an ode of Horace: he may have been a mathematician, but he will not sit down to work out an equation; he will leap at once from the sinking vessel into the boat, for his object will be to save his life. And should it not be so as to his eternal life? My soul, my soul, this must be saved, and with all my heart will I seek to God in Jesus Christ that I may find salvation.

The text further adds that we are to turn to Him. Did you notice the thirtieth verse—"*If thou turn to the Lord thy God*." It must be a thorough turn.

You are looking now toward the world—you must turn in the opposite direction, and look Godward. It must not be an apparent turn, but a real change of the nature, a turning of the entire soul; a turning with repentance for the past, with confidence in Christ for the present, and with holy desires for the future. Heart, soul, life, speech, action, all must be changed. Except you be converted you cannot enter the kingdom of heaven. May God grant you such a turn as this, and to this end do you pray, "Turn me, and I shall be turned."

Then it is added, "*and be obedient to his voice*," for we cannot be saved in disobedience; Christ is not come to save His people in their sins, but from their sins. "If ye be willing and obedient, ye shall eat the good of the land: but if ye refuse and rebel, ye shall be devoured with the sword." Do you see, my dear unconverted hearers, what God's advice is to you? It is that now you obey His Gospel, and bow before the scepter of His Son Jesus. He would have you own that you have erred, and entreat to be kept from erring again. Your proud self-will must yield, and your self-confidence must be renounced, and you must incline your ear and come to Him, "Hear and your soul shall live." This His Holy Spirit will grant you grace to do. This is the least that could be asked of you; you could not expect the great King to pardon rebels and allow them to continue in rebellion. He could not allow you to continue in sin and yet partake of His grace. You know that such a course would not be worthy of a holy God.

Do you feel inclined at this moment to turn to the Lord? Does some gentle power you have never felt before draw you beyond yourself? Do you perceive that it would be well for you to be reconciled to your God and Father? Do you feel some kindlings of regret, some sparks of good desire? Then yield to the impulse; I trust it is the Holy Spirit within, working in you to will and to do of His own good pleasure. Yield at once; completely yield, and He will lead you by a way you know not, and bring you to Jesus, and in Him you shall find peace and rest, holiness, happiness, and heaven. Let this be the happy day. Bend before the Spirit's breath as the reed bows in the wind. Quench not the Spirit, grieve Him no more—

> Lest slighted once the season fair
> Should ne'er return again.

Beware lest bleeding love should never woo again, lest pitying grace should never more entreat, and tender mercy should never more cast its cords around you. The spouse said, "Draw me, we will run after thee," do you say the same. Behold, before you there is an open door, and within that door a waiting Savior; will you perish on the threshold?

Very Rich Encouragements

Thirdly, the text contains very rich encouragements. How does it run?

"For the Lord thy God is a merciful God; *he will not forsake thee.*" Catch at that sinner, "He will not forsake thee." If He were to say. "Let him alone, Ephraim is given unto idols," it would be all over with you; but if you seek Him He will not say, "Let him alone," nor take His Holy Spirit from you. You are not yet given up, I hope, or you would not have been here this morning to hear this sermon.

I thought when I woke this morning, and saw the snow and pitiless sleet driven by a vehement wind, that it was a pity I had studied such a subject, for I would like to have the house crowded with sinners, and they are not so likely to come out in bad weather. Just then I recollected that it was upon just such a morning as this that I found the Savior myself, and that thought gave me much courage in coming here. I thought the congregation cannot be smaller than that of which I made one on that happy day when I looked to Christ. I believe that many will this morning be bought out and saved, for the Lord has not forsaken this congregation. I used to think He had given me up, and would not show me mercy after so long seeking in vain; but He had not forsaken *me*, nor has He cast *you* off, O sinner! If you seek Him with all your heart, you may rest assured He will not forsake you.

And then it is added, *"Neither destroy thee."* You have been afraid He would; you have often thought the earth would open and swallow you; you have been afraid to fall asleep lest you should never wake again; but the Lord will not destroy you; nay rather He will reveal His saving power in you.

There is a sweeter word still in verse 29: *"Thou shalt find him if thou seek him."* I wish I could sing, and could extemporize a bit of music, for then I would stand here and sing those words: "Thou shalt find him if thou seek him." At any rate, the words have sweet melody in them to my ear and heart—"Thou shalt find him if thou seek him." I would like to whisper that sentence softly to the sick, and to shout it to the busy. It ought to linger long in your memories, and abide in your hearts—"Thou shalt find him if thou seek him." What more, poor sinner, what more do you want?

Then there are two reasons given: *"For the Lord thy God is a merciful God."* Oh, guilty soul, the Lord does not want to damn you, He does not desire to destroy you. Judgment is His strange work. Have you ever had to chasten your child? When you have felt bound to punish severely by reason of a great fault, has it not been very hard work? You have said to yourself a hundred times over, "What shall I do? What shall I do to escape from the misery of causing pain to my dear child?" You have been driven to chasten him or you would not have done it. God never sends a sinner to hell until justice demands it. He finds no joy in punishing. He swears, "As I live, saith the Lord, I have no pleasure in the death of him that dieth." Look at the judge when he puts on the black cap, does he do so with pleasure? Nay, some of our judges speak with choked utterance and with many tears when they say to the prisoner, "You must be taken to the place from whence you came, there to be hanged by the neck until you are dead." God never puts on the black cap without His heart yearning for men. His mercy endures forever, and he delights in it.

Notice how the Lord teaches us His care even over the most guilty by the comparisons He makes. "What man of you," says He, "having a sheep gone astray will not go after it until he find it? What man of you having a sheep that is fallen into a ditch will not pull it out?" Any animal which belongs to us causes us concern if we lose it, or it is in trouble. I noticed the other night how even the little kitten could not be missing without causing anxiety to the household. What calling and searching! Rougher natures might say, "If the kitten will keep out of doors all night, let it do so." But the owner thought not so, for the night was cold and wet. I have seen great trouble when a bird has been lost through the opening of a cage door, and many a vain struggle to catch it again. What a stir there is in the house about a little short-lived animal. We do not like to lose a bird, or a kitten, and do you think the good God will willingly lose those whom He has made in His own image, and who are to exist forever? I have used a very simple and homely illustration, but it commends itself to the heart. You know what you would do to regain a lost bird, and what will not God do to save a soul! An immortal spirit is better than ten thousand birds. Does God care for souls? Ay, that He does, and in proof thereof Jesus has come to seek and to save the lost. The shepherd cannot rest while one of his flock is in danger. "It is only one sheep! You have ninety-nine more, good man, why do you fret and bother yourself about one?" He cannot be pacified. He is considering where that sheep may be. He imagines all sorts of perils and distresses. Perhaps it is lying on its back, and cannot turn over, or it has fallen into a pit, or is entangled among briars, or the wolf is ready to seize it. It is not merely its intrinsic value to him, but he is concerned for it because it *his* sheep, and the object of his care. Oh, soul, God has such a care for man. He waits to be gracious, and His Spirit goes forth toward sinners; therefore return to Him.

Now dwell upon that last argument—"*He will not forget the covenant of thy fathers.*" The covenant always keeps open the path between God and man. The Lord has made a covenant concerning poor sinners with His Son Jesus Christ. He has laid help upon one that is mighty, and given Him for a covenant to the people. He evermore remembers Jesus, and how He kept that covenant; He calls to mind His sighs, and tears, and groans, and death-throes, and He fulfills His promise for the great Sufferer's sake. God's grace has kept His covenant on the behalf of men; God is even eager to forgive that He may reward Christ, and give Him to see of the travail of His soul. Now, hearken to me, you who are still unconverted. What solid ground there is here for your hope. If the Lord were to deal with you according to the covenant of works, what could He do but destroy you? But there is a covenant of grace made in Jesus Christ on the behalf of sinners, and all that believe in Jesus are interested in that covenant and are made partakers of the countless blessings which that covenant secures. Believe in Jesus. Cast yourself upon Him, and by the covenant mercies of God you shall assuredly be saved.

You have heard me preach like this before, have you not, a good many times? Yes, and I am sometimes fearful lest God's people should grow tired of this kind of sermon, but then *you* need it over and over again. How many more times will some of you want to be told this? How many more times must the great mercy of God be set before you? Are we to keep on inviting you again and again and again, and go back with no favorable answer from you? I have been questioning myself in the night watches about this, and I have said, "These people are unconverted, is it my fault? Do I fail in telling them my Lord's message? Do I mar the Gospel?" Well, I thought, "If it be so, yet I will charge them not to be partakers of my fault." Brothers and sisters, God's mercy is so rich that, even when the story of it is badly told, it ought to influence your hearts. It is so grand a thing that God should be in Christ reconciling the world to Himself by a wondrous sacrifice, that if I stuttered and stammered you ought to be glad to hear it; or even if I told you in terms that were obscure you ought to be so eager to know it that you would search out my meaning. In secret correspondence a cipher is often use, but inquisitive people soon discover it; ought there not to be yet more interest taken in the Gospel? But, my friends, I do not speak obscurely. I am as plain a speaker as one might meet in a day's march, and with all my heart I set Christ before you, and bid you trust Him; will you do so this morning, or will you not? See how dark it is outside, even at noonday. God has hung the very heavens in mourning. Never fear, the sun will soon break forth and light up the day; and even so

> Our hearts, if God we seek to know
> Shall know him, and rejoice;
> Him coming like the morn shall be,
> As morning songs his voice.
>
> So shall his presence bless our souls,
> And shed a joyful light;
> That hallow'd morn shall chase away
> The sorrows of the night.